CW00517213

The Big

Air Fryer Cookbook UK

Simple and Budget-Friendly Recipes incl.Side Dishes, Desserts and More to Maximise the Use of Your Air Fryer

Brittni G. Brock

Copyright© 2022 By Brittni G. Brock All Rights Reserved

This book is copyright protected. It is only for personal use. You cannot amend, distribute, sell, use, quote or paraphrase any part of the content within this book, without the consent of the author or publisher.

Under no circumstances will any blame or legal responsibility be held against the publisher, or author, for any damages, reparation, or monetary loss due to the information contained within this book, either directly or indirectly.

Disclaimer Notice:

Please note the information contained within this document is for educational and entertainment purposes only. All effort has been executed to present accurate, up to date, reliable, complete information. No warranties of any kind are declared or implied. Readers acknowledge that the author is not engaged in the rendering of legal, financial, medical or professional advice. The content within this book has been derived from various sources. Please consult a licensed professional before attempting any techniques outlined in this book.

By reading this document, the reader agrees that under no circumstances is the author responsible for any losses, direct or indirect, that are incurred as a result of the use of the information contained within this document, including, but not limited to, errors, omissions, or inaccuracies.

Contents

Introduction

Chapter 1 Fast and Easy Everyday Favourites

Chapter 2 Staples, Sauces, Dips, and Dressings

Chapter 3 Poultry

Chapter 4 Fish and Seafood

Chapter 5 Vegetarian Mains

Chapter 6 Vegetables and Sides

Chapter 7 Pizzas, Wraps, and Sandwiches

Chapter 8 Desserts

Introduction

There is a fair probability that you are familiar with air fryers. This kitchen gadget has been around for a while and is now a staple in every home. It can make almost no-oil French fries, chicken nuggets, vegetable cutlets, and Indian deep-fried appetizers like samosas, vadas, and kachoris. Additionally, it is a terrific kitchen tool and my go-to for cooking leftovers like chicken drumsticks, which typically go soggy when heated in a microwave.

I was sceptical when I used the air fryer for the first time, just like you probably are. I didn't have much room in my kitchen, and this was just another thing that would take up valuable counter space while most likely not being used very frequently. I was sure I'd regret it; however, I got one.

It turns out that I was completely off base. I use my air fryer for almost everything now because I not only adore it but also because I used to bake most things in the oven. Although it does take some space, its permanent position on my tabletop serves as a reminder to use it and ensures that most days, I don't even need to open the oven. It's helpful.

I've used Air fryers to bake bread, cakes, doughnuts, and other baked goods in addition to deep-fried foods. It works just as well in assisting you in preparing delectable meals. Place your sides inside the air fryer and let it handle the cooking if you have the main course you would like to spend much more time preparing. The air fryer produces delicious results with vegetables such as asparagus, Broccoli, potatoes, zucchini, sprouts & onions, and cauliflower.

In a considerably smaller package, it provides all the convenience and adaptability of an OTG (Oven Toaster Griller). It reduces calorie and fat intake without sacrificing the crunch and flavour we all enjoy. Given the variety of possibilities, it is simple to become perplexed if you are thinking about purchasing one. Therefore, we have put together this guide to help you find the best air fryer for your kitchen.

What Are Air Fryers

An air fryer is a small tabletop oven that uses convection principles to fry food without submerging it in oil. It stimulates the process of frying using convection as its method of heat transfer compared to the common use of radiation with ovens. Cooking quick, delicious, and healthful dishes in your home has been easier thanks to innovative kitchen appliances like the air fryer. I've noticed it helps save a lot of my time, yes, and I'll also reduce the amount of oil in my food, which is much more significant.

An air fryer can be likened to the regular oven, given that it bakes and roasts food, it differs from an oven in that it uses less oil and has heating elements that are only placed at the top. As a result, food in an air fryer becomes extremely crispy quickly. Owing to the implementation of a focused source of heat as well as the size combined with the positioning of the fan, air fryers often heat up pretty quickly and make meals quickly and effectively.

The Maillard reaction occurs when foods are completely submerged in heated oil with temperature levels between 140 and 165 °C (284 and 329 °F), which is above the water's boiling temperature. Next, the food is coated in a light coating of hot oil and heated to 200 °C (392 °F), the maximum temperature an air fryer can reach.

High heat and a powerful fan are used in air fryers to bake food. The preheat period is virtually nonexistent, meaning that it hardly requires you to preheat it; from the moment you turn it on, it gets hot almost immediately. Air fryers also use little, if any, oil. This is so that the food can come out crisp and succulent, but the flavour differs from what you might expect.

Before using an air fryer for cooking items that have been battered, the oil must be sprayed over the food to aid its colour and become crispy. However, it is important to remember that moist and flour-based recipes don't cook evenly in an air fryer.

Most air fryers enable temperature level and timer adjustments, which facilitate more accurate cooking. Usually, cooking takes place in baskets that rest on a drip tray. Whether through a manual process or using the fryer mechanism, the basket needs to be stirred up from time to time. While air fryers and convection ovens cook food similarly, air fryers typically are smaller and produce less heat.

Air Fryers can also prepare food much more quickly and frequently more evenly thanks to their small size and intense heat source with a fan. A practical approach to speed up meal preparation, especially for families usually occupied with work, is to use the air fryer. Many of them also demand little, if any, preheating time.

How To Choose An Air Fryer

When picking an air Fryer, it is important to note the main purpose and what you would be using it for. Many things stand out for me, but I've handpicked some for you.

1. Volume and size

Size is a crucial consideration, especially if your kitchen is small. The capacity of a medium-sized air fryer ranges from 3.7L to 4.1L. They should readily fit in most kitchens because they are tiny. However, size and capacity have a direct relationship. If you have a big family or host lots of parties, choosing a small or medium-sized fryer may force you to cook food in batches, which you don't want to do. Larger air fryers can cook food more rapidly for more people, but they also tend to be bulkier, so make your choice carefully.

2. Controls

Dials on air fryers often control the temperature and timer. Look for more expensive ones with digital controls if you want greater precision. They also include LED displays to display information and allow you to set specific settings. Additionally, to simplify the cooking process, some air fryers offer presets. Additionally, you should search for a newly emerging class of smart air fryers. Thanks to their Wi-Fi connectivity, you can set cooking modes directly from your phone.

3. Cleaning

It's crucial to thoroughly clean your air fryer regularly. Fortunately, cleaning an air fryer doesn't take much effort. Simply remove its drawer and wash it with the faucet on. A dishwashing detergent can completely wash the inner basket, which is frequently removable. The nonstick coating on these baskets typically keeps the food from sticking. Additionally, some models come with a dishwasher-safe design.

Healthy food may be prepared quickly and easily in air fryers without sacrificing flavour. Most chefs advise cutting the cooking or baking time by 20% because it cooks food more quickly. For instance, if the original recipe calls for conventional cooking for 30 minutes, air frying for 24 minutes ought to suffice. Users also require temperature settings so they can prevent overcooking.

4. Features for safety

Which kinds of security measures does it have? For example, does it have an auto-shutoff? I always want to confirm if it has these features. You should ensure the Air Fryer has various safety features like auto-shutoff and a cool touch exterior because it gets very hot as it heats up.

Just be certain when choosing one because the majority will have these features. Always read customer reviews before making a purchase. If you are searching online, browse them, read the products with positive reviews, and consider the advantages and disadvantages. By doing this, you'll locate one quickly that matches your demands and possibly even discover some fresh recipe suggestions.

What Can You Cook In An Air Fryer And What Foods To Avoid?

After getting your Air Fryer, maybe you've had your air Fryer sitting in a corner for a long time; I understand you're dying to try your hands on some recipes, or you're wondering what you could cook with your Air Fryer. Below is a list of some of my most recommended foods to cook:

Grilled Salmon

Use your air fryer to prepare fish in the shortest time ever; with a fantastic top crust and great inside tenderness and flakiness, the salmon cooks in about 10 minutes. Of course, the sweet mustard topping elevates this, but you are welcome to use your preferred marinade here too.

Goat Cheese, Spinach, And Roasted Red Pepper Omelette Cooked In The Air Fryer

The main capabilities of the air fryer are well demonstrated by this omelette packed with vegetables. Next, create your omelette bar at home by customizing the fillings. Hot tip: The omelette will

appear set on top before it's finished cooking. If the egg on the bottom is still runny when you remove it from your air fryer, so you fold it, then simply put it back in for some more time.

Pork Chops

We don't usually get very enthused about pork chops. Frequently overcooked, they turn out dry, depressing, and flavourless. However, everything changes when you cook the pork in the air fryer. The high heat circulation results in a minor crisping of the surface while maintaining a luscious interior.

Chicken Parmesan

It is Incredible (not to mention how rapidly the air fryer can accomplish it!) because crispy golden chicken can be produced without the need for any oil. There is no need to heat your oven or create a big mess of oil on your stovetop: There is significantly less work involved in making this chicken Parm, and it tastes just as excellent as the classic dish.

Sweet Potato Hash Air Fried

These potatoes are infused with smoked paprika with dill, making them the perfect savoury breakfast food. Adapt the spices to what is in the cupboard (chilli powder is a great option). Even though this meal is filling on its own, you may up the power by topping it with a poached egg or a scoop of Greek yoghurt.

Some Foods To Avoid Cooking With Your Air Fryer

Foods with a moist batter

This is because there won't be enough heated oil to properly set the batter, and it will probably drip instead of forming a crunchy coating.

Popcorn

This well-known movie treat won't cook effectively in your air fryer either because most models won't get hot enough to make the kernels pop.

What Are The Advantages Of Air Fryers

Below are some reasons why Air Fryers are much better choices and their benefits;

- Servicing Is Not a Big Deal
- The mess that kitchen equipment can produce while cooking is among their worst aspects, making the cleaning procedure difficult. But thanks to advancements in air frying technology, the damage to the equipment after frying is minimal.
- Air Frying is much safer than Deep Frying
- Foods are deep-fried by heating a big container of hot oil. This might be dangerous. Even though air fryers eventually get hot, there is no danger of spills, splatters, or unintentional touching
- Losing weight can be aided by using air fryers.
- Increased intake of fried meals is directly linked to an increased risk of obesity. This is so that people don't consume too many calories and fat from deep-fried dishes. Weight loss

can be aided by switching to air-fried foods instead of deep-fried ones and consuming fewer unhealthy oils regularly.

- User-Friendly
- Unlike some other kitchen equipment, utilizing the air fryer is relatively straightforward. It wouldn't take you lots of guidance to figure out how to utilize it on your own. All you need to understand is how to insert the cut meat or potato pieces into the basket because the mechanism is simple. Once finished, simply set the cooking device to cook, and the task will be completed quickly.
- Reducing the consumption of fried foods lowers illness risk
- Numerous harmful health issues have been linked too frequently using oil in cooking and eating traditional fried dishes. One can lessen the risk of developing these issues by substituting alternate cooking techniques for deep frying.
- Air fryers lessen the possibility of hazardous acrylamide production.
- Cooking food in oil can lead to the formation of hazardous substances like acrylamide. When foods are cooked at high heat, like deep frying, this chemical develops in some foods. According to the International Agency for Research on Cancer, acrylamide may be related to the development of several malignancies, including endometrial, ovarian, pancreatic, breast, and oesophageal cancer. Additional investigations Although the results are inconclusive, they have also suggested a connection between dietary acrylamide and renal, endometrial, or ovarian malignancies.

How To Clean & Maintain Air Fryers

I will be sharing my tips on keeping my Air Fryers clean, and I hope you can emulate and take on these steps too. So here's my meticulously curated list.

- Switch off your air fryer.
- Let the air fryer elements get to room temperature first if you've just finished cooking.
- Take the basket away
- Let each basket rest in warm water with soap for ten to fifteen minutes.
- Try washing the basket with a non-abrasive brush while the warm water and soap solution are still inside if there is caked-on grease or difficult-to-remove stains.
- To clean the air fryer's interior, use a wet cloth or sponge and a little dish soap.
- The heating element should be cleaned with a sponge or cloth by turning the air fryer upside down.
- Making a paste of baking soda and water and using a soft-bristled brush to scrape away any remaining residue is another option for tough stains.
- Allow the air fryer parts to cool

The Care Tips With Air Fryers

Oil up your Air Fryer Basket
Often take a little time to lubricate your air fryer

basket, even though your food doesn't call for oil. I oil mine by rubbing, or squirting, just that little smidge of oil, mostly on the bottom grates. It will make sure the food doesn't stick.

Don't ever use aerosol cans in the air fryer

Aerosol spray containers (like Pam and similar brands) are popular for causing chipping in many Air Fryer baskets. The spray cans have harsh ingredients that won't blend with the coat over most baskets. It's advised to make expenses in a nice quality oil canister or bottle. I am well acquainted with the Evo Spray Bottle.

You will regret waiting to clean.

Don't put it off. Ciufo advises not letting food scraps and crumbs lie in the basket or drawer overnight to avoid a cleaning nightmare. "After you've finished cooking, disconnect the air fryer, let it cool, remove the oil from where it usually is, the pullout drawer, then discard it." Cleaning the grate, basket, and drawer while they are still heated can make it simpler to remove any sticky sauce from the item you are air-frying, such as marinated ribs.

How to Handle Persistent Odors

Even after cleaning, your air fryer may still smell strong when a food releases a strong odour when cooking. The food basket and drawer should be soaked in warm water and detergent for between 30 and 60 minutes until cleaning again, advises NewAir, the company that makes Magic Chef air fryers. If the fragrance still exists, cut a lemon in halves, rub it across the basket and the drawer, and then rewash after 30 minutes.

Take Care When Using Nonstick

Customers have expressed dissatisfaction with the nonstick covering on certain air fryer parts flaking off over time on our website and elsewhere. Although we haven't observed this (our tests assess performance immediately out of the box), our advice for other nonstick kitchenware is still applicable here: Avoid using steel wool, metal utensils, and every other abrasive since they can damage the nonstick coating by scratching or chipping it.

Also, avoid using the air fryer if the nonstick covering is peeling. Instead, request a new basket over the phone from the manufacturer's customer care or return the air fryer to the shop.

Frequently Asked Questions

1. Do I need to buy more items or accessories for my air fryer?

Racks and pans are included with certain air fryers. While these have their uses, our recipes in Air Fryer Perfection were developed to only use the standard air fryer basket. Therefore, there is no need for additional bells and whistles.

2. How to define an air fryer?

Air fryers are big tabletop equipment that flawlessly cooks food with very little oil (typically less than a tablespoon). However, despite its nice name, air fryers are not fryers.

3. Is deep frying unhealthy, or is air frying?

We discovered that the top air fryers created food

much better than oven-fried alternatives and considerably healthier than deep-fried selections.

4. What is the capacity of an air fryer?

Depending on how much the food might be, most standard air fryers can fit 2 to 4 servings of food. So it's crucial to avoid stuffing the basket too full.

5. Do I need to warm the air fryer?

An air fryer warms considerably quicker than the average oven. When using a cold air fryer, starting food to cook took the same time as waiting to allow the air fryer to heat up.

6. How can I keep my air fryer from getting clogged with food?

For types of food predisposed to sticking, like breaded chicken or tender fish, we strongly advise squirting the basket delicately with vegetable oil aerosol. You can also use a foil sling.

7. How else do I cleanse my air fryer?

Most removable elements of said air fryer, including the drawer and basket of several models, are easy to clean. Still, you must review your air-fryer handbook before placing parts inside the dishwasher.

8. What should I do? Should I smell the smoke during air frying, or if the smell coming from my air fryer change?

Clean the air fryer! Researchers found the most serious difficulties with smoking and odour due to an unclean air fryer. Make careful to thoroughly clean the area everywhere in the air fryer's heating element to get rid of any accumulated residue if you notice a lot of smoke and smell of burnt. However, your food hasn't burned.

Chapter 1 Fast and Easy Everyday Favourites

Simple and Easy Croutons

Prep time: 5 minutes / Cook time: 8 minutes
Serves 4

Ingredients :

- 2 slices bread
- 1 tablespoon olive oil
- Hot soup, for serving

Preparation Instructions :

1. Preheat the air fryer to 200°C.
2. Cut the slices of bread into medium-size chunks.
3. Brush the air fryer basket with the oil.
4. Place the chunks inside and air fry for at least 8 minutes.
5. Serve with hot soup.

Scalloped Veggie Mix

Prep time: 10 minutes / Cook time: 15 minutes
Serves 4

Ingredients :

- 1 Yukon Gold or other small white potato, thinly sliced
- 1 small sweet potato, peeled and thinly sliced
- 1 medium carrot, thinly sliced
- 60 ml minced onion
- 3 garlic cloves, minced
- 180 ml 2 percent milk
- 2 tablespoons cornflour
- ½ teaspoon dried thyme

Preparation Instructions :

1. Preheat the air fryer to 192°C.
2. In a baking pan, layer the potato, sweet potato, carrot, onion, and garlic.
3. In a small bowl, whisk the milk, cornflour, and thyme until blended.
4. Pour the milk mixture evenly over the vegetables in the pan. Bake for 15 minutes.
5. Check the casserole—it should be golden brown on top, and the vegetables should be tender. Serve immediately.

Cheesy Potato Patties

Prep time: 5 minutes / Cook time: 10 minutes
Serves 8

Ingredients :

- 900 g white potatoes
- 120 ml finely chopped spring onions
- ½ teaspoon freshly ground black pepper, or more to taste
- 1 tablespoon fine sea salt
- ½ teaspoon hot paprika
- 475 ml shredded Colby or Monterey Jack cheese
- 60 ml rapeseed oil
- 235 ml crushed crackers

Preparation Instructions :

1. Preheat the air fryer to 182°C.
2. Boil the potatoes until soft. Dry them off and peel them before mashing thoroughly, leaving no lumps.
3. Combine the mashed potatoes with spring onions, pepper, salt, paprika, and cheese. Mould the mixture into balls with your hands and press with your palm to flatten them into patties.
4. In a shallow dish, combine the rapeseed oil and crushed crackers. Coat the patties in the crumb mixture.
5. Bake the patties for about 10 minutes, in multiple batches if necessary.
6. Serve hot.

Baked Chorizo Scotch Eggs

Prep timeBaked Chorizo
Scotch Eggs

Ingredients :

- 450 g Mexican chorizo or other seasoned sausage meat
- 4 soft-boiled eggs plus 1 raw egg
- 1 tablespoon water
- 120 ml plain flour
- 235 ml panko breadcrumbs
- Cooking spray

Preparation Instructions :

1. Divide the chorizo into 4 equal portions. Flatten each portion into a disc.
2. Place a soft-boiled egg in the centre of each disc. Wrap the chorizo around the egg, encasing it

completely. Place the encased eggs on a plate and chill for at least 30 minutes.

3. Preheat the air fryer to 182°C.

4. Beat the raw egg with 1 tablespoon of water.

5. Place the flour on a small plate and the panko on a second plate.

6. Working with 1 egg at a time, roll the encased egg in the flour, then dip it in the egg mixture. Dredge the egg in the panko and place on a plate.

7. Repeat with the remaining eggs.

8. Spray the eggs with oil and place in the air fryer basket. Bake for 10 minutes.

9. Turn and bake for an additional 5 to 10 minutes, or until browned and crisp on all sides. Serve immediately.

Cheesy Baked Grits

Prep time: 10 minutes / Cook time: 12 minutes
Serves 6

Ingredients :

- 180 ml hot water
- 2 (28 g) packages instant grits
- 1 large egg, beaten
- 1 tablespoon butter, melted
- 2 cloves garlic, minced
- ½ to 1 teaspoon red pepper flakes
- 235 ml shredded Cheddar cheese or jalapeño Jack cheese

Preparation Instructions :

1. Preheat the air fryer to 204°C.

2. In a baking pan, combine the water, grits, egg, butter, garlic, and red pepper flakes. Stir until well combined.

3. Stir in the shredded cheese. Place the pan in the air fryer basket and air fry for 12 minutes, or until the grits have cooked through and a knife inserted near the centre comes out clean.

4. Let stand for 5 minutes before serving.

Cheesy Chilli Toast

Prep time: 5 minutes / Cook time: 5 minutes
Serves 1

Ingredients :

- 2 tablespoons grated Parmesan cheese
- 2 tablespoons grated Mozzarella cheese
- 2 teaspoons salted butter, at room temperature

- 10 to 15 thin slices serrano chilli or jalapeño
- 2 slices sourdough bread
- ½ teaspoon black pepper

Preparation Instructions :

1. Preheat the air fryer to 164°C.
2. In a small bowl, stir together the Parmesan, Mozzarella, butter, and chillies.
3. Spread half the mixture onto one side of each slice of bread. Sprinkle with the pepper.
4. Place the slices, cheese-side up, in the air fryer basket. Bake for 5 minutes, or until the cheese has melted and started to brown slightly.
5. Serve immediately..

Sweet Corn and Carrot Fritters

Prep time: 10 minutes / Cook time: 8 to 11 minutes
Serves 4

Preparation Instructions :

1. Preheat the air fryer to 176°C.
2. Place the grated carrot in a colander and press down to squeeze out any excess moisture. Dry it with a paper towel.
3. Combine the carrots with the remaining ingredients. Mould 1 tablespoon of the mixture into a ball and press it down with your hand or a spoon to flatten it.
4. Repeat until the rest of the mixture is used up.
5. Spritz the balls with cooking spray. Arrange in the air fryer basket, taking care not to overlap any balls. Bake for 8 to 11 minutes, or until they're firm.
6. Serve warm.

Beery and Crunchy Onion Rings

Prep time: 10 minutes / Cook time: 16 minutes
Serves 2 to 4

Ingredients :

- 160 ml plain flour
- ½ teaspoon bicarbonate of soda
- ½ teaspoon freshly ground black pepper
- 180 ml beer
- 1 tablespoons olive oil
- 1 teaspoon paprika
- 1 teaspoon salt
- 1 egg, beaten
- 350 ml breadcrumbs
- Cooking spray
- 1 large Vidalia or sweet onion, peeled and sliced into ½-inch rings

Preparation Instructions :

1. Preheat the air fryer to 182°C. Spritz the air fryer basket with cooking spray.

2. Combine the flour, paprika, bicarbonate of soda, salt, and ground black pepper in a bowl. Stir to mix well.
3. Combine the egg and beer in a separate bowl. Stir to mix well. Make a well in the centre of the flour mixture, then pour the egg mixture in the well. Stir to mix everything well.
4. Pour the breadcrumbs and olive oil in a shallow plate. Stir to mix well.
5. Dredge the onion rings gently into the flour and egg mixture, then shake the excess off and put into the plate of breadcrumbs. Flip to coat both sides well.
6. Arrange the onion rings in the preheated air fryer. Air fry in batches for 16 minutes or until golden brown and crunchy. Flip the rings and put the bottom rings to the top halfway through.
7. Serve immediately.

Buttery Sweet Potatoes

Prep time: 5 minutes / Cook time: 10 minutes
Serves 4

Ingredients :

- 2 tablespoons butter, melted
- 1 tablespoon light brown sugar
- 2 sweet potatoes, peeled and cut into ½-inch cubes
- Cooking spray

Preparation Instructions :

Preheat the air fryer to 204°C. Line the air fryer basket with parchment paper. In a medium bowl, stir together the melted butter and brown sugar until blended. Toss the sweet potatoes in the butter mixture until coated. Place the sweet potatoes on the parchment and spritz with oil. Air fry for 5 minutes. Shake the basket, spritz the sweet potatoes with oil, and air fry for 5 minutes more until they're soft enough to cut with a fork. Serve immediately.

Baked Cheese Sandwich

Prep time: 5 minutes / Cook time: 8 minutes
Serves 2

Ingredients :

- 2 tablespoons mayonnaise
- 4 thick slices sourdough bread
- 4 thick slices Brie cheese
- 8 slices hot capicola or prosciutto

Preparation Instructions :

1. Preheat the air fryer to 204°C. Line the air fryer basket with parchment paper.

2. In a medium bowl, stir together the melted butter and brown sugar until blended.
3. Toss the sweet potatoes in the butter mixture until coated. Place the sweet potatoes on the parchment and spritz with oil. Air fry for 5 minutes.
4. Shake the basket, spritz the sweet potatoes with oil, and air fry for 5 minutes more until they're soft enough to cut with a fork.
5. Serve immediately.

Baked Halloumi with Greek Salsa

Prep timeBaked Halloumi with Greek Salsa

Salsa:
- 1 small shallot, finely diced
- 2 tablespoons fresh lemon juice
- 1 teaspoon freshly cracked black pepper
- 120 ml finely diced English cucumber
- 2 teaspoons chopped fresh parsley
- 1 teaspoon snipped fresh oregano
- 3 garlic cloves, minced
- 2 tablespoons extra-virgin olive oil
- Pinch of rock salt
- 1 plum tomato, deseeded and finely diced
- 1 teaspoon snipped fresh dill

Cheese:
- 227 g Halloumi cheese, sliced into ½-inch-thick pieces
- 1 tablespoon extra-virgin olive oil

Preparation Instructions :

Preheat the air fryer to 192°C.

For the salsa:

Combine the shallot, garlic, lemon juice, olive oil, pepper, and salt in a medium bowl. Add the cucumber, tomato, parsley, dill, and oregano. Toss gently to combine; set aside.

For the cheese:

Place the cheese slices in a medium bowl. Drizzle with the olive oil. Toss gently to coat. Arrange the cheese in a single layer in the air fryer basket. Bake for 6 minutes. Divide the cheese among four serving plates. Top with the salsa and serve immediately.

Herb-Roasted Veggies

Prep time: 10 minutes / Cook time: 14 to 18 minutes
Serves 4

Ingredients :
- 1 red pepper, sliced
- 235 ml green beans, cut into 2-inch pieces
- 3 garlic cloves, sliced
- ½ teaspoon dried basil
- 1 (230 g) package sliced mushrooms
- 80 ml diced red onion
- 1 teaspoon olive oil
- ½ teaspoon dried tarragon

Preparation Instructions :

1. Preheat the air fryer to 176ºC.
2. In a medium bowl, mix the red pepper, mushrooms, green beans, red onion, and garlic. Drizzle with the olive oil. Toss to coat.
2. Add the herbs and toss again.
3. Place the vegetables in the air fryer basket. Roast for 14 to 18 minutes, or until tender.
4. Serve immediately.

Rosemary and Orange Roasted Chickpeas

Prep time: 5 minutes / Cook time: 10 to 12 minutes
Makes 1 L

Ingredients :

- 1 L cooked chickpeas
- 1 teaspoon rock salt
- 1 teaspoon paprika
- 1 tablespoon chopped fresh rosemary
- 2 tablespoons vegetable oil
- 1 teaspoon cumin
- Zest of 1 orange

Preparation Instructions :

1. Preheat the air fryer to 204ºC.
2. Make sure the chickpeas are completely dry prior to roasting. In a medium bowl, toss the chickpeas with oil, salt, cumin, and paprika.
3. Working in batches, spread the chickpeas in a single layer in the air fryer basket. Air fry for 10 to 12 minutes until crisp, shaking once halfway through.
4. Return the warm chickpeas to the bowl and toss with the orange zest and rosemary.
5. Allow to cool completely. Serve.

Corn Fritters

Prep time: 15 minutes / Cook time: 8 minutes
Serves 6

Ingredients :

- 235 ml self-raising flour
- 1 teaspoon salt
- 60 ml buttermilk
- 60 ml minced onion
- 1 tablespoon sugar
- 1 large egg, lightly beaten
- 180 ml corn kernels
- Cooking spray

Preparation Instructions :

1. Preheat the air fryer to 176ºC.
2. Line the air fryer basket with parchment paper.

3. In a medium bowl, whisk the flour, sugar, and salt until blended. Stir in the egg and buttermilk. Add the corn and minced onion. Mix well.
4. Shape the corn fritter batter into 12 balls.
5. Place the fritters on the parchment and spritz with oil. Bake for 4 minutes. Flip the fritters, spritz them with oil, and bake for 4 minutes more until firm and lightly browned.
6. Serve immediately.

Bacon Pinwheels

Prep time: 10 minutes / Cook time: 10 minutes
Makes 8 pinwheels

Ingredients :

- 1 sheet puff pastry
- 2 tablespoons maple syrup
- 60 ml brown sugar
- 8 slices bacon
- Ground black pepper, to taste
- Cooking spray

Preparation Instructions :

1. Preheat the air fryer to 182°C.
2. Spritz the air fryer basket with cooking spray.
3. Roll the puff pastry into a 10-inch square with a rolling pin on a clean work surface, then cut the pastry into 8 strips.
4. Brush the strips with maple syrup and sprinkle with sugar, leaving a 1-inch far end uncovered. Arrange each slice of bacon on each strip, leaving a ⅛-inch length of bacon hang over the end close to you. Sprinkle with black pepper.
5. From the end close to you, roll the strips into pinwheels, then dab the uncovered end with water and seal the rolls.
6. Arrange the pinwheels in the preheated air fryer and spritz with cooking spray. Air fry for 10 minutes or until golden brown. Flip the pinwheels halfway through.
7. Serve immediately.

Gochujang Dip

Prep time: 5 minutes / Cook time: 0 minutes
Serves 4

Ingredients :

- 2 tablespoons gochujang (Korean red pepper paste)
- 1 tablespoon mayonnaise
- 1 tablespoon toasted sesame oil
- 1 tablespoon minced fresh ginger
- 1 tablespoon minced garlic
- 1 teaspoon agave nectar

Preparation Instructions :

1. In a small bowl, combine the gochujang, mayonnaise, sesame oil, ginger, garlic, and agave. Stir until well combined.
2. Use immediately or store in the refrigerator, covered, for up to 3 days.

Red Buffalo Sauce

Prep time: 5 minutes / Cook time: 20 minutes
Makes 475 ml

Ingredients :

- 60 ml olive oil
- 4 garlic cloves, roughly chopped
- 1 (142 g) small red onion, roughly chopped
- 6 red chillies, roughly chopped (about 56 g in total)
- 235 ml water
- 120 ml apple cider vinegar
- ½ teaspoon salt
- ½ teaspoon freshly ground black pepper

Preparation Instructions :

1. In a large non-stick sauté pan, heat 60 ml olive oil over medium-high heat. Once it's hot, add the garlic, onion, and chillies. Cook for 5 minutes, stirring occasionally, until onions are golden brown.
2. Add the water and bring to a boil. Cook for about 10 minutes or until the water has nearly evaporated.

3. Transfer the cooked onion and chili mixture to a food processor or blender and blend briefly to combine.
4. Add the apple cider vinegar, salt, and pepper. Blend again for 30 seconds.
5. Using a mesh sieve, strain the sauce into a bowl. Use a spoon or spatula to scrape and press all the liquid from the pulp.

Tomatillo Salsa for Air Fryer

Prep time: 5 minutes / Cook time: 15 minutes
Serves 4

Ingredients :

- 12 tomatillos or alternatively underripe tomatoes with a dash of lime juice
- 2 fresh serrano chillies or jalapeños
- 1 tablespoon minced garlic
- 235 ml chopped fresh coriander leaves
- 1 tablespoon vegetable oil
- 1 teaspoon rock salt

Preparation Instructions :

1. Remove and discard the papery husks from the tomatillos and rinse them under warm running water to remove the sticky coating.
2. Place the tomatillos and peppers in a baking pan. Place the pan in the air fryer basket. Air fry at 176°C for 15 minutes.
3. Transfer the tomatillos and peppers to a blender, add the garlic, coriander, vegetable oil, and salt, and blend until almost smooth. (If not using immediately, omit the salt and add it just before serving.)
4. Serve or store in an airtight container in the refrigerator for up to 10 days.

Hot Honey Mustard Dip

Prep time: 5 minutes / Cook time: 0 minutes
Makes 315 ml

Ingredients :

- 180 ml mayonnaise
- 80 ml spicy brown mustard
- 60 ml honey
- ½ teaspoon cayenne pepper

Preparation Instructions :

1. In a medium bowl, stir together the mayonnaise, mustard, and honey until blended. Stir in the cayenne.

2.Cover and chill for 3 hours so the flavours blend. Keep refrigerated in an airtight container for up to 3 weeks.

Pepper Sauce

Prep time: 10 minutes / Cook time: 20 minutes
Makes 1 L

Ingredients :

- 2 red hot fresh chillies, seeded
- 2 dried chillies
- ½ small brown onion, roughly chopped
- 2 garlic cloves, peeled
- 475 ml water
- 475 ml white vinegar

Preparation Instructions :

1.In a medium saucepan, combine the fresh and dried chillies, onion, garlic, and water.
2.Bring to a simmer and cook for 20 minutes, or until tender.
3.Transfer to a food processor or blender. Add the vinegar and blend until smooth.

Mushroom Apple Gravy

Prep time: 5 minutes / Cook time: 10 minutes
Serves 4

Ingredients :

- 475 ml vegetable broth
- 120 ml finely chopped mushrooms
- 2 tablespoons wholemeal flour
- 1 tablespoon unsweetened apple sauce
- 1 teaspoon onion powder
- ½ teaspoon dried thyme
- ¼ teaspoon dried rosemary
- ⅛ teaspoon pink Himalayan salt
- Freshly ground black pepper, to taste

Preparation Instructions :

1.In a non-stick saucepan over medium-high heat, combine all the ingredients and mix well.
2.Bring to a boil, stirring frequently, reduce the heat to low, and simmer, stirring constantly, until it thickens.

Cashew Mayo

Prep time: 5 minutes / Cook time: 0 minutes
Makes 18 tablespoons

Ingredients :

- 235 ml cashews, soaked in hot water for at least 1 hour
- 60 ml plus 3 tablespoons milk
- 1 tablespoon apple cider vinegar
- 1 tablespoon freshly squeezed lemon juice
- 1 tablespoon Dijon mustard
- 1 tablespoon aquafaba or egg alternative
- ⅛ teaspoon pink Himalayan salt

Preparation Instructions :

In a food processor, combine all the ingredients and blend until creamy and smooth.

Apple Cider Dressing

Prep time: 5 minutes / Cook time: 0 minutes
Serves 2

Ingredients :

- 2 tablespoons apple cider vinegar
- ⅓ lemon, zested
- ⅓ lemon, juiced
- Salt and freshly ground black pepper, to taste

Preparation Instructions :

1. In a jar, combine the vinegar, lemon juice, and zest.
2. Season with salt and pepper, cover, and shake well.

Dijon and Balsamic Vinaigrette

Prep time: 5 minutes / Cook time: 0 minutes
Makes 12 tablespoons

Ingredients :

- 6 tablespoons water
- 4 tablespoons Dijon mustard
- 4 tablespoons balsamic vinegar
- 1 teaspoon maple syrup
- ½ teaspoon pink Himalayan salt
- ¼ teaspoon freshly ground black pepper

Preparation Instructions :

In a bowl, whisk together all the ingredients.

Pecan Tartar Sauce

Prep time: 10 minutes / Cook time: 10 minutes
Makes 300 ml

Ingredients :

- 4 tablespoons pecans, finely chopped
- 120 ml sour cream
- 120 ml mayonnaise
- ½ teaspoon grated lemon zest
- 1½ tablespoons freshly squeezed lemon juice
- 2½ tablespoons chopped fresh parsley
- 1 teaspoon paprika
- 2 tablespoons chopped dill pickle

Preparation Instructions :

1. Preheat the air fryer to 164ºC.
2. Spread the pecans in a single layer on a parchment sheet lightly spritzed with oil. Place the pecans in the air fryer. Air fry for 7 to 10 minutes, stirring every 2 minutes. Let cool.
3. In a medium bowl, mix the sour cream, mayonnaise, lemon zest, and lemon juice until blended. Stir in the parsley paprika, dill pickle, and pecans.
4. Cover and refrigerate to chill for at least 1 hour to blend the flavours.
5. This sauce should be used within 2 weeks.

Cajun-Breaded Chicken Bites

Prep time: 10 minutes / Cook time: 12 minutes
Serves 4

Ingredients :

- 450 g boneless, skinless chicken breasts, cut into 1-inch cubes
- 120 g heavy whipping cream
- ½ teaspoon salt
- ¼ teaspoon ground black pepper
- 30 g plain pork rinds, finely crushed
- 40 g unflavoured whey protein powder
- ½ teaspoon Cajun seasoning

Preparation Instructions :

1. Place chicken in a medium bowl and pour in cream. Stir to coat. Sprinkle with salt and pepper.
2. In a separate large bowl, combine pork rinds, protein powder, and Cajun seasoning. Remove chicken from cream, shaking off any excess, and toss in dry mix until fully coated.
3. Place bites into ungreased air fryer basket. Adjust the temperature to 200°C and air fry for 12 minutes, shaking the basket twice during cooking. Bites will be done when golden brown and have an internal temperature of at least 76°C. Serve warm.

French Garlic Chicken

Prep time: 30 minutes / Cook time: 27 minutes
Serves 4

Ingredients :

- 2 tablespoon extra-virgin olive oil
- 1 tablespoon Dijon mustard
- 1 tablespoon apple cider vinegar
- 3 cloves garlic, minced
- 2 teaspoons herbes de Provence
- ½ teaspoon kosher salt
- 1 teaspoon black pepper
- 450 g boneless, skinless chicken thighs, halved crosswise
- 2 tablespoons butter
- 8 cloves garlic, chopped
- 60 g heavy whipping cream

Preparation Instructions :

1. In a small bowl, combine the olive oil, mustard, vinegar, minced garlic, herbes de Provence, salt, and pepper. Use a wire whisk to emulsify the mixture.

2. Pierce the chicken all over with a fork to allow the marinade to penetrate better. Place the chicken in a resealable plastic bag, pour the marinade over, and seal. Massage until the chicken is well coated. Marinate at room temperature for 30 minutes or in the refrigerator for up to 24 hours.

3. When you are ready to cook, place the butter and chopped garlic in a baking pan and place it in the air fryer basket. Set the air fryer to 200°C for 5 minutes, or until the butter has melted and the garlic is sizzling.

4. Add the chicken and the marinade to the seasoned butter. Set the air fryer to 180°C for 15 minutes. Use a meat thermometer to ensure the chicken has reached an internal temperature of 76°C. Transfer the chicken to a plate and cover lightly with foil to keep warm.

5. Add the cream to the pan, stirring to combine with the garlic, butter, and cooking juices. Place the pan in the air fryer basket. Set the air fryer to 180°C for 7 minutes.

6. Pour the thickened sauce over the chicken and serve.

Chicken Chimichangas

Prep time: 20 minutes / Cook time: 8 to 10 minutes
Serves 4

Ingredients :

- 280 g cooked chicken, shredded
- ½ teaspoon oregano
- ½ teaspoon onion powder
- Salt and pepper, to taste
- Oil for misting or cooking spray

- 2 tablespoons chopped green chilies
- ½ teaspoon cumin
- ¼ teaspoon garlic powder
- 8 flour tortillas (6- or 7-inch diameter)

Chimichanga Sauce:

- 2 tablespoons butter
- 235 ml chicken broth
- ¼ teaspoon salt
- 60 g Pepper Jack or Monterey Jack cheese, shredded

- 2 tablespoons flour
- 60 g light sour cream

Preparation Instructions :

1. Make the sauce by melting butter in a saucepan over medium-low heat. Stir in flour until smooth and slightly bubbly. Gradually add broth, stirring constantly until smooth. Cook and stir 1 minute, until the mixture slightly thickens. Remove from heat and stir in sour cream and salt. Set aside.

2. In a medium bowl, mix together the chicken, chilies, oregano, cumin, onion powder, garlic, salt, and pepper. Stir in 3 to 4 tablespoons of the sauce, using just enough to make the filling moist but not soupy.

3. Divide filling among the 8 tortillas. Place filling down the centre of tortilla, stopping about 1

inch from edges. Fold one side of tortilla over filling, fold the two sides in, and then roll up. Mist all sides with oil or cooking spray.

4. Place chimichangas in air fryer basket seam side down. To fit more into the basket, you can stand them on their sides with the seams against the sides of the basket.

5. Air fry at 180°C for 8 to 10 minutes or until heated through and crispy brown outside.

6. Add the shredded cheese to the remaining sauce. Stir over low heat, warming just until the cheese melts. Don't boil or sour cream may curdle.

7. Drizzle the sauce over the chimichangas.

Crunchy Chicken Tenders

Prep time: 5 minutes / Cook time: 12 minutes
Serves 4

Ingredients :

- 1 egg
- 30 g whole wheat flour
- ½ teaspoon salt
- ½ teaspoon dried thyme
- ½ teaspoon garlic powder
- 1 lemon, quartered
- 60 ml unsweetened almond milk
- 30 g whole wheat bread crumbs
- ½ teaspoon black pepper
- ½ teaspoon dried sage
- 450 g chicken tenderloins

Preparation Instructions :

1. Preheat the air fryer to 184°C.
2. In a shallow bowl, beat together the egg and almond milk until frothy.
3. In a separate shallow bowl, whisk together the flour, bread crumbs, salt, pepper, thyme, sage, and garlic powder.
4. Dip each chicken tenderloin into the egg mixture, then into the bread crumb mixture, coating the outside with the crumbs. Place the breaded chicken tenderloins into the bottom of the air fryer basket in an even layer, making sure that they don't touch each other.
5. Cook for 6 minutes, then turn and cook for an additional 5 to 6 minutes. Serve with lemon slices.

Harissa-Rubbed Chicken

Prep time: 30 minutes / Cook time: 21 minutes
Serves 4

Ingredients :

Harissa:

- 120 ml olive oil
- 2 tablespoons smoked paprika
- 1 tablespoon ground cumin
- 1 teaspoon kosher salt
- 6 cloves garlic, minced
- 1 tablespoon ground coriander
- 1 teaspoon ground caraway
- ½ to 1 teaspoon cayenne pepper

Chickens:
- 120 g yogurt
- 2 small chickens, any giblets removed, split in half lengthwise

Preparation Instructions :

1. For the harissa: In a medium microwave-safe bowl, combine the oil, garlic, paprika, coriander, cumin, caraway, salt, and cayenne. Microwave on high for 1 minute, stirring halfway through the cooking time. (You can also heat this on the stovetop until the oil is hot and bubbling. Or, if you must use your air fryer for everything, cook it in the air fryer at 180°C for 5 to 6 minutes, or until the paste is heated through.)

2. For the chicken: In a small bowl, combine 1 to 2 tablespoons harissa and the yogurt. Whisk until well combined. Place the chicken halves in a resealable plastic bag and pour the marinade over. Seal the bag and massage until all of the pieces are thoroughly coated. Marinate at room temperature for 30 minutes or in the refrigerator for up to 24 hours.

3. Arrange the hen halves in a single layer in the air fryer basket. (If you have a smaller air fryer, you may have to cook this in two batches.) Set the air fryer to 200°C for 20 minutes. Use a meat thermometer to ensure the chickens have reached an internal temperature of 76°C.

Crispy Dill Chicken Strips

Prep time: 30 minutes / Cook time: 10 minutes
Serves 4

Ingredients :

- 2 whole boneless, skinless chicken breasts (about 450 g each), halved lengthwise
- 230 ml Italian dressing
- 110 g finely crushed crisps
- 1 tablespoon dried dill weed
- 1 tablespoon garlic powder
- 1 large egg, beaten
- 1 to 2 tablespoons oil

Preparation Instructions :

1. In a large resealable bag, combine the chicken and Italian dressing. Seal the bag and refrigerate to marinate at least 1 hour.

2. In a shallow dish, stir together the potato chips, dill, and garlic powder. Place the beaten egg in a second shallow dish.

3. Remove the chicken from the marinade. Roll the chicken pieces in the egg and the crisp mixture, coating thoroughly.

4. Preheat the air fryer to 170°C. Line the air fryer basket with parchment paper.

5. Place the coated chicken on the parchment and spritz with oil.

6. Cook for 5 minutes. Flip the chicken, spritz it with oil, and cook for 5 minutes more until the outsides are crispy and the insides are no longer pink.

Bruschetta Chicken

Prep time: 10 minutes / Cook time: 20 minutes
Serves 4

Ingredients :

Bruschetta Stuffing:
- 1 tomato, diced
- 3 tablespoons balsamic vinegar
- 1 teaspoon Italian seasoning
- 2 tablespoons chopped fresh basil
- 3 garlic cloves, minced
- 2 tablespoons extra-virgin olive oil

Chicken:
- 4 (115 g) boneless, skinless chicken breasts, cut 4 slits each
- 1 teaspoon Italian seasoning
- Chicken seasoning or rub, to taste
- Cooking spray

Preparation Instructions :

1. Preheat the air fryer to 190°. Spritz the air fryer basket with cooking spray.
2. Combine the ingredients for the bruschetta stuffing in a bowl. Stir to mix well. Set aside.
3. Rub the chicken breasts with Italian seasoning and chicken seasoning on a clean work surface.
4. Arrange the chicken breasts, slits side up, in a single layer in the air fryer basket and spritz with cooking spray. You may need to work in batches to avoid overcrowding.
5. Air fry for 7 minutes, then open the air fryer and fill the slits in the chicken with the bruschetta stuffing. Cook for another 3 minutes or until the chicken is well browned.
6. Serve immediately.

Chicken and Ham Meatballs with Dijon Sauce

Prep time: 10 minutes / Cook time: 15 minutes
Serves 4

Ingredients :

Meatballs:
- 230 g ham, diced
- 110 g grated Swiss cheese
- 3 cloves garlic, minced
- 1½ teaspoons sea salt
- Cooking spray
- 230 g chicken mince
- 1 large egg, beaten
- 15 g chopped onions
- 1 teaspoon ground black pepper

Dijon Sauce:

- 3 tablespoons Dijon mustard
- 60 ml chicken broth, warmed
- ¼ teaspoon ground black pepper
- 2 tablespoons lemon juice
- ¾ teaspoon sea salt
- Chopped fresh thyme leaves, for garnish

Preparation Instructions :

1. Preheat the air fryer to 200°C. Spritz the air fryer basket with cooking spray.
2. Combine the ingredients for the meatballs in a large bowl. Stir to mix well, then shape the mixture in twelve 1½-inch meatballs.
3. Arrange the meatballs in a single layer in the air fryer basket. Air fry for 15 minutes or until lightly browned. Flip the balls halfway through. You may need to work in batches to avoid overcrowding.
4. Meanwhile, combine the ingredients, except for the thyme leaves, for the sauce in a small bowl. Stir to mix well.
5. Transfer the cooked meatballs on a large plate, then baste the sauce over. Garnish with thyme leaves and serve.

Personal Cauliflower Pizzas

Prep time: 10 minutes / Cook time: 25 minutes
Serves 2

Ingredients :

- 1 (340 g) bag frozen riced cauliflower
- 25 g almond flour
- 1 large egg
- 1 teaspoon garlic powder
- 75 g shredded Mozzarella cheese
- 20 g Parmesan cheese
- ½ teaspoon salt
- 1 teaspoon dried oregano
- 4 tablespoons no-sugar-added marinara sauce, divided
- 110 g fresh Mozzarella, chopped, divided
- 140 g cooked chicken breast, chopped, divided
- 100 g chopped cherry tomatoes, divided
- 5 g fresh baby rocket, divided

Preparation Instructions :

1. Preheat the air fryer to 200°C. Cut 4 sheets of parchment paper to fit the basket of the air fryer. Brush with olive oil and set aside.
2. In a large glass bowl, microwave the cauliflower according to package directions. Place the cauliflower on a clean towel, draw up the sides, and squeeze tightly over a sink to remove the excess moisture. Return the cauliflower to the bowl and add the shredded Mozzarella along with the almond flour, Parmesan, egg, salt, garlic powder, and oregano. Stir until thoroughly combined.
3. Divide the dough into two equal portions. Place one piece of dough on the prepared parchment

paper and pat gently into a thin, flat disk 7 to 8 inches in diameter. Air fry for 15 minutes until the crust begins to brown. Let cool for 5 minutes.

4. Transfer the parchment paper with the crust on top to a baking sheet. Place a second sheet of parchment paper over the crust. While holding the edges of both sheets together, carefully lift the crust off the baking sheet, flip it, and place it back in the air fryer basket. The new sheet of parchment paper is now on the bottom. Remove the top piece of paper and air fry the crust for another 15 minutes until the top begins to brown. Remove the basket from the air fryer.

5. Spread 2 tablespoons of the marinara sauce on top of the crust, followed by half the fresh Mozzarella, chicken, cherry tomatoes, and rocket. Air fry for 5 to 10 minutes longer, until the cheese is melted and beginning to brown. Remove the pizza from the oven and let it sit for 10 minutes before serving. Repeat with the remaining ingredients to make a second pizza.

Ethiopian Chicken with Cauliflower

Prep time: 15 minutes / Cook time: 28 minutes
Serves 6

Ingredients :

- 2 handful fresh Italian parsley, roughly chopped
- 2 sprigs thyme
- 1½ small-sized head cauliflower, broken into large-sized florets
- 2 teaspoons mustard powder
- 1½ teaspoons berbere spice
- ½ teaspoon shallot powder
- 1 teaspoon freshly cracked pink peppercorns
- 20 g fresh chopped chives
- 6 chicken drumsticks
- ⅓ teaspoon porcini powder
- ⅓ teaspoon sweet paprika
- 1 teaspoon granulated garlic
- ½ teaspoon sea salt

Preparation Instructions :

1. Simply combine all items for the berbere spice rub mix. After that, coat the chicken drumsticks with this rub mix on all sides. Transfer them to the baking dish.

2. Now, lower the cauliflower onto the chicken drumsticks. Add thyme, chives and Italian parsley and spritz everything with a pan spray. Transfer the baking dish to the preheated air fryer.

3. Next step, set the timer for 28 minutes; roast at 180°C, turning occasionally. Bon appétit!

Peanut Butter Chicken Satay

Prep time: 12 minutes / Cook time: 12 to 18 minutes
Serves 4

Ingredients :

- 120 g crunchy peanut butter
- 3 tablespoons low-sodium soy sauce
- 80 ml chicken broth
- 2 tablespoons freshly squeezed lemon juice

- 2 garlic cloves, minced
- 1 teaspoon curry powder
- Cooking oil spray
- 2 tablespoons extra-virgin olive oil
- 450 g chicken tenders

Preparation Instructions :

1. In a medium bowl, whisk the peanut butter, broth, soy sauce, lemon juice, garlic, olive oil, and curry powder until smooth.
2. Place 2 tablespoons of this mixture into a small bowl. Transfer the remaining sauce to a serving bowl and set aside.
3. Add the chicken tenders to the bowl with the 2 tablespoons of sauce and stir to coat. Let stand for a few minutes to marinate.
4. Insert the crisper plate into the basket and the basket into the unit. Preheat the unit by selecting AIR FRY, setting the temperature to 200ºC, and setting the time to 3 minutes. Select START/ STOP to begin.
5. Run a 6-inch bamboo skewer lengthwise through each chicken tender.
6. Once the unit is preheated, spray the crisper plate with cooking oil. Working in batches, place half the chicken skewers into the basket in a single layer without overlapping.
7. Select AIR FRY, set the temperature to 200ºC, and set the time to 9 minutes. Select START/ STOP to begin.
8. After 6 minutes, check the chicken. If a food thermometer inserted into the chicken registers 76ºC, it is done. If not, resume cooking.
9. Repeat steps 6, 7, and 8 with the remaining chicken. 10. When the cooking is complete, serve the chicken with the reserved sauce.

Chicken with Lettuce

Prep time: 15 minutes / Cook time: 14 minutes
Serves 4

Ingredients :

- 450 g chicken breast tenders, chopped into bite-size pieces
- ½ onion, thinly sliced
- ½ red bell pepper, seeded and thinly sliced
- ½ green bell pepper, seeded and thinly sliced
- 1 tablespoon olive oil
- 1 tablespoon fajita seasoning
- 1 teaspoon kosher salt
- Juice of ½ lime
- 8 large lettuce leaves
- 230 g prepared guacamole

Preparation Instructions :

1. Preheat the air fryer to 200ºC.
2. In a large bowl, combine the chicken, onion, and peppers. Drizzle with the olive oil and toss until thoroughly coated. Add the fajita seasoning and salt and toss again.
3. Working in batches if necessary, arrange the chicken and vegetables in a single layer in the air fryer basket. Pausing halfway through the cooking time to shake the basket, air fry for 14 minutes, or until the vegetables are tender and a thermometer inserted into the thickest piece of chicken registers 76ºC.
4. Transfer the mixture to a serving platter and drizzle with the fresh lime juice. Serve with the lettuce leaves and top with the guacamole.

Fajita-Stuffed Chicken Breast

Prep time: 15 minutes / Cook time: 25 minutes
Serves 4

Ingredients :

- 2 (170 g) boneless, skinless chicken breasts
- ¼ medium white onion, peeled and sliced
- 1 medium green bell pepper, seeded and sliced
    - 1 tablespoon coconut oil
- 2 teaspoons chili powder
- 1 teaspoon ground cumin
- ½ teaspoon garlic powder

Preparation Instructions :

1. Slice each chicken breast completely in half lengthwise into two even pieces. Using a meat tenderizer, pound out the chicken until it's about ¼-inch thickness.
2. Lay each slice of chicken out and place three slices of onion and four slices of green pepper on the end closest to you. Begin rolling the peppers and onions tightly into the chicken. Secure the roll with either toothpicks or a couple pieces of butcher's twine.
3. Drizzle coconut oil over chicken. Sprinkle each side with chili powder, cumin, and garlic powder. Place each roll into the air fryer basket.
4. Adjust the temperature to 180ºC and air fry for 25 minutes.
5. Serve warm.

Tex-Mex Chicken Breasts

Prep time: 10 minutes / Cook time: 17 to 20 minutes
Serves 4

Ingredients :

- 450 g low-sodium boneless, skinless chicken breasts, cut into 1-inch cubes
- 1 medium onion, chopped
- 1 red bell pepper, chopped
- 1 jalapeño pepper, minced
- 2 teaspoons olive oil
- 115 g canned low-sodium black beans, rinsed and drained
- 130 g low-sodium salsa
- 2 teaspoons chili powder

Preparation Instructions :

1. Preheat the air fryer to 200°C.
2. In a medium metal bowl, mix the chicken, onion, bell pepper, jalapeño, and olive oil. Roast for 10 minutes, stirring once during cooking.
3. Add the black beans, salsa, and chili powder. Roast for 7 to 10 minutes more, stirring once, until the chicken reaches an internal temperature of 76°C on a meat thermometer. Serve immediately.

Chicken Legs with Leeks

Prep time: 30 minutes / Cook time: 18 minutes
Serves 6

Ingredients :

- 2 leeks, sliced
- 2 large-sized tomatoes, chopped
- 3 cloves garlic, minced
- ½ teaspoon dried oregano
- 6 chicken legs, boneless and skinless
- ½ teaspoon smoked cayenne pepper
- 2 tablespoons olive oil
- A freshly ground nutmeg

Preparation Instructions :

1. In a mixing dish, thoroughly combine all ingredients, minus the leeks. Place in the refrigerator and let it marinate overnight.
2. Lay the leeks onto the bottom of the air fryer basket. Top with the chicken legs.
3. Roast chicken legs at (190°C for 18 minutes, turning halfway through. Serve with hoisin sauce.

Trout Amandine with Lemon Butter Sauce

Prep time: 20 minutes / Cook time:8 minutes
Serves 4

Ingredients :

Trout Amandine:
- 65 g toasted almonds
- 1 teaspoon salts
- 2 tablespoons butter, melteds
- Cooking spray

- 30 g grated Parmesan cheese
- ½ teaspoon freshly ground black pepper
- 4 trout fillets, or salmon fillets, 110 g each

Lemon Butter Sauce:
- 8 tablespoons butter, melteds
- ½ teaspoon Worcestershire sauces
- ½ teaspoon freshly ground black pepper

- 2 tablespoons freshly squeezed lemon juice
- ½ teaspoon salt
- ¼ teaspoon hot sauce

Preparation Instructions :

1. In a blender or food processor, pulse the almonds for 5 to 10 seconds until finely processed. Transfer to a shallow bowl and whisk in the Parmesan cheese, salt, and pepper. Place the melted butter in another shallow bowl.
2. One at a time, dip the fish in the melted butter, then the almond mixture, coating thoroughly.
3. Preheat the air fryer to 150ºC. Line the air fryer basket with baking paper.
4. Place the coated fish on the baking paper and spritz with oil.
5. Bake for 4 minutes. Flip the fish, spritz it with oil, and bake for 4 minutes more until the fish flakes easily with a fork.
6. In a small bowl, whisk the butter, lemon juice, Worcestershire sauce, salt, pepper, and hot sauce until blended.
7. Serve with the fish.

Prawn Kebabs

Prep time: 15 minutes / Cook time: 6 minutes
Serves 4

Ingredients :

- Olive or vegetable oil, for spraying
- 455 g medium raw prawns, peeled and deveined
- 4 tablespoons unsalted butter, melted
- 1 tablespoon Old Bay seasoning

- 1 tablespoon packed light brown sugar
- 1 teaspoon granulated garlic
- 1 teaspoon onion powder
- ½ teaspoon freshly ground black pepper

Preparation Instructions :

1. Line the air fryer basket with baking paper and spray lightly with oil.
2. Thread the prawns onto the skewers and place them in the prepared basket.
3. In a small bowl, mix together the butter, Old Bay, brown sugar, garlic, onion powder, and black pepper. Brush the sauce on the prawns.
4. Air fry at 204°C for 5 to 6 minutes, or until pink and firm. Serve immediately.

Breaded Prawns Tacos

Prep time: 10 minutes / Cook time: 9 minutes
Makes 8 tacos

Ingredients :

- 2 large eggss
- 1 teaspoon prepared yellow mustard
- 455 g small prawns, peeled, deveined, and tails removed
- 45 g finely shredded Gouda or Parmesan cheese
- 80 g pork scratchings ground to dusts
- For Serving:
- 8 large round lettuce leavess
- 60 ml pico de gallo
- 20 g shredded purple cabbages
- 1 lemon, sliced
- Guacamole (optional)

Preparation Instructions :

1. Preheat the air fryer to 204°C.
2. Crack the eggs into a large bowl, add the mustard, and whisk until well combined. Add the prawns and stir well to coat.
3. In a medium-sized bowl, mix together the cheese and pork scratching dust until well combined.
4. One at a time, roll the coated prawns in the pork scratching dust mixture and use your hands to press it onto each prawns. Spray the coated prawns with avocado oil and place them in the air fryer basket, leaving space between them.
5. Air fry the prawns for 9 minutes, or until cooked through and no longer translucent, flipping after 4 minutes.
6. To serve, place a lettuce leaf on a serving plate, place several prawns on top, and top with 1½ teaspoons each of pico de gallo and purple cabbage. Squeeze some lemon juice on top and serve with guacamole, if desired.
7. Store leftover prawns in an airtight container in the refrigerator for up to 3 days. Reheat in a preheated 204°C air fryer for 5 minutes, or until warmed through.

Tuna Nuggets in Hoisin Sauce

Prep time: 15 minutes / Cook time: 5 to 7 minutes
Serves 4

Ingredients :

- 120 ml hoisin sauces
- 2 teaspoons sesame oils
- 2 teaspoons dried lemongrasss
- ½ small onion, quartered and thinly sliced
- Cooking sprays
- 2 tablespoons rice wine vinegar
- 1 teaspoon garlic powder
- ¼ teaspoon red pepper flakes
- 230 g fresh tuna, cut into 1-inch cubes
- 560 g cooked jasmine rice

Preparation Instructions :

1. Mix the hoisin sauce, vinegar, sesame oil, and seasonings together.
2. Stir in the onions and tuna nuggets.
3. Spray a baking pan with nonstick spray and pour in tuna mixture.
4. Roast at 200°C for 3 minutes. Stir gently.
5. Cook 2 minutes and stir again, checking for doneness. Tuna should be barely cooked through, just beginning to flake and still very moist. If necessary, continue cooking and stirring in 1-minute intervals until done.
6. Serve warm over hot jasmine rice.

Cayenne Sole Cutlets

Prep time: 15 minutes / Cook time: 10 minutes
Serves 2

Ingredients :

- 1 egg
- 120 g Pecorino Romano cheese, grated
- Sea salt and white pepper, to taste
- ½ teaspoon cayenne pepper
- 1 teaspoon dried parsley flakes
- 2 sole fillets

Preparation Instructions :

1. To make a breading station, whisk the egg until frothy.
2. In another bowl, mix Pecorino Romano cheese, and spices.
3. Dip the fish in the egg mixture and turn to coat evenly; then, dredge in the cracker crumb mixture, turning a couple of times to coat evenly.
4. Cook in the preheated air fryer at 200°C for 5 minutes; turn them over and cook another 5 minutes. Enjoy!

Orange-Mustard Glazed Salmon

Prep time: 10 minutes / Cook time: 10 minutes
Serves 2

Ingredients :

- 1 tablespoon orange marmalade
- ¼ teaspoon grated orange zest plus 1 tablespoon juice
- 2 teaspoons whole-grain mustard
- 2 (230 g) skin-on salmon fillets, 1½ inches thick
- Salt and pepper, to taste
- Vegetable oil spray

Preparation Instructions :

1. Preheat the air fryer to 204ºC.
2. Make foil sling for air fryer basket by folding 1 long sheet of aluminum foil so it is 4 inches wide. Lay sheet of foil widthwise across basket, pressing foil into and up sides of basket. Fold excess foil as needed so that edges of foil are flush with top of basket. Lightly spray foil and basket with vegetable oil spray.
3. Combine marmalade, orange zest and juice, and mustard in bowl. Pat salmon dry with paper towels and season with salt and pepper. Brush tops and sides of fillets evenly with glaze. Arrange fillets skin side down on sling in prepared basket, spaced evenly apart. Air fry salmon until center is still translucent when checked with the tip of a paring knife and registers 52ºC (for medium-rare), 10 to 14 minutes, using sling to rotate fillets halfway through cooking.
4. Using the sling, carefully remove salmon from air fryer. Slide fish spatula along underside of fillets and transfer to individual serving plates, leaving skin behind. Serve.

Prawn and Cherry Tomato Kebabs

Prep time: 15 minutes / Cook time: 5 minutes
Serves 4

Ingredients :

- 680 g jumbo prawns, cleaned, peeled and deveined
- 2 tablespoons butter, melteds
- Sea salt and ground black pepper, to tastes
- ½ teaspoon dried basils
- ½ teaspoon mustard seedss
- 455 g cherry tomatoes
- 1 tablespoons Sriracha sauce
- 1 teaspoon dried parsley flakes
- ½ teaspoon dried oregano
- ½ teaspoon marjoram

Special Equipment:

- 4 to 6 wooden skewers, soaked in water for 30 minutes

Preparation Instructions :

1. Preheat the air fryer to 204ºC.

2. Put all the ingredients in a large bowl and toss to coat well.
3. Make the kebabs: Thread, alternating jumbo prawns and cherry tomatoes, onto the wooden skewers that fit into the air fryer.
4. Arrange the kebabs in the air fryer basket. You may need to cook in batches depending on the size of your air fryer basket.
5. Air fry for 5 minutes, or until the prawns are pink and the cherry tomatoes are softened. Repeat with the remaining kebabs. Let the prawns and cherry tomato kebabs cool for 5 minutes and serve hot.

Apple Cider Mussels

Prep time: 10 minutes / Cook time: 2 minutes
Serves 5

Ingredients :

- 900 g mussels, cleaned and de-beardeds
- 1 teaspoon ground cumin s
- 60 ml apple cider vinegar
- 1 teaspoon onion powder
- 1 tablespoon avocado oil

Preparation Instructions :

1. Mix mussels with onion powder, ground cumin, avocado oil, and apple cider vinegar.
2. Put the mussels in the air fryer and cook at 202°C for 2 minutes.

Prawns Pasta with Basil and Mushrooms

Prep time: 10 minutes / Cook time: 10 minutes
Serves 6

Ingredients :

- 455 g small prawns, peeled and deveineds
- ¼ teaspoon garlic powders
- 455 g whole grain pastas
- 230 g baby mushrooms, sliceds
- 1 teaspoon salts
- ½ cup fresh basil
- 120 ml olive oil plus 1 tablespoon, divided
- ¼ teaspoon cayenne
- 5 garlic cloves, minced
- 45 g Parmesan, plus more for serving (optional)
- ½ teaspoon black pepper

Preparation Instructions :

1. Preheat the air fryer to 192°C.
2. In a small bowl, combine the prawns, 1 tablespoon olive oil, garlic powder, and cayenne. Toss to coat the prawns.
3. Place the prawns into the air fryer basket and roast for 5 minutes. Remove the prawns and set

aside.

4. Cook the pasta according to package directions. Once done cooking, reserve ½ cup pasta water, then drain.

5. Meanwhile, in a large skillet, heat 120 ml of olive oil over medium heat. Add the garlic and mushrooms and cook down for 5 minutes.

6. Pour the pasta, reserved pasta water, Parmesan, salt, pepper, and basil into the skillet with the vegetable-and-oil mixture, and stir to coat the pasta.

7. Toss in the prawns and remove from heat, then let the mixture sit for 5 minutes before serving with additional Parmesan, if desired.

Air Fried Crab Bun

Prep time: 15 minutes / Cook time: 20 minutes
Serves 2

Ingredients :

- 140 g crab meat, chopped s
- 2 tablespoons coconut flour s
- ½ teaspoon coconut aminos, or tamari s
- 1 tablespoon coconut oil, softened

- 2 eggs, beaten
- ¼ teaspoon baking powder
- ½ teaspoon ground black pepper

Preparation Instructions :

1. In the mixing bowl, mix crab meat with eggs, coconut flour, baking powder, coconut aminos, ground black pepper, and coconut oil.
2. Knead the smooth dough and cut it into pieces.
3. Make the buns from the crab mixture and put them in the air fryer basket.
4. Cook the crab buns at 185ºC for 20 minutes.

Mackerel with Spinach

Prep time: 15 minutes / Cook time: 20 minutes
Serves 5

Ingredients :

- 455 g mackerel, trimmed s
- 15 g spinach, chopped s
- 1 teaspoon ground black pepper s

- 1 bell pepper, chopped
- 1 tablespoon avocado oil
- 1 teaspoon tomato paste

Preparation Instructions :

1. In the mixing bowl, mix bell pepper with spinach, ground black pepper, and tomato paste.
2. Fill the mackerel with spinach mixture.
3. Then brush the fish with avocado oil and put it in the air fryer.

4. Cook the fish at 185°C for 20 minutes.

Prawns with Swiss Chard

Prep time: 10 minutes / Cook time: 10 minutes
Serves 4

Ingredients :

- 455 g prawns, peeled and deveined s
- 70 g Swiss chard, chopped s
- 1 tablespoon coconut oil s
- ½ teaspoon smoked paprika
- 2 tablespoons apple cider vinegar
- 60 ml heavy cream

Preparation Instructions :

1. Mix prawns with smoked paprika and apple cider vinegar.
2. Put the prawns in the air fryer and add coconut oil.
3. Cook the prawns at 176°C for 10 minutes.
4. Then mix cooked prawns with remaining ingredients and carefully mix.

South Indian Fried Fish

Prep time: 20 minutes / Cook time: 8 minutes
Serves 4

Ingredients :

- 2 tablespoons olive oils
- 1 teaspoon minced fresh gingers
- 1 teaspoon ground turmerics
- ¼ to ½ teaspoon cayenne peppers
- Olive oil sprays
- 2 tablespoons fresh lime or lemon juice
- 1 clove garlic, minced
- ½ teaspoon kosher or coarse sea salt
- 455 g tilapia fillets (2 to 3 fillets)
- Lime or lemon wedges (optional)

Preparation Instructions :

1. In a large bowl, combine the oil, lime juice, ginger, garlic, turmeric, salt, and cayenne. Stir until well combined; set aside.
2. Cut each tilapia fillet into three or four equal-size pieces. Add the fish to the bowl and gently mix until all of the fish is coated in the marinade. Marinate for 10 to 15 minutes at room temperature. (Don't marinate any longer or the acid in the lime juice will "cook" the fish.)
3. Spray the air fryer basket with olive oil spray. Place the fish in the basket and spray the fish. Set the air fryer to 164°C for 3 minutes to partially cook the fish. Set the air fryer to 204°C for 5 minutes to finish cooking and crisp up the fish. (Thinner pieces of fish will cook faster so you may want to check at the 3-minute mark of the second cooking time and remove those that are cooked through, and then add them back toward the end of the second cooking time to crisp.)
4. Carefully remove the fish from the basket. Serve hot, with lemon wedges if desired.

Tilapia with Pecans

Prep time: 20 minutes / Cook time: 16 minutes
Serves 5

Ingredients :

- 2 tablespoons ground flaxseedss
- Sea salt and white pepper, to taste s
- 2 tablespoons extra-virgin olive oil s
- 5 tilapia fillets, sliced into halves
- 1 teaspoon paprika
- 1 teaspoon garlic paste
- 65 g pecans, ground

Preparation Instructions :

1. Combine the ground flaxseeds, paprika, salt, white pepper, garlic paste, olive oil, and ground pecans in a sealable freezer bag. Add the fish fillets and shake to coat well.
2. Spritz the air fryer basket with cooking spray. Cook in the preheated air fryer at 204°C for 10 minutes; turn them over and cook for 6 minutes more. Work in batches.
3. Serve with lemon wedges, if desired. Enjoy!

Lemon-Dill Salmon Burgers

Prep time: 10 minutes / Cook time: 8 minutes
Serves 4

Ingredients :

- 2 fillets of salmon, 170 g each, finely chopped by hand or in a food processor
- 150 g fine bread crumbss
- 2 tablespoons chopped fresh dill s
- Freshly ground black pepper, to tastes
- 4 brioche or hamburger buns
- Lettuce, tomato, red onion, avocado, mayonnaise or mustard, for serving
- 1 teaspoon freshly grated lemon zest
- 1 teaspoon salt
- 2 eggs, lightly beaten

Preparation Instructions :

1. Preheat the air fryer to 204°C.
2. Combine all the ingredients in a bowl. Mix together well and divide into four balls. Flatten the balls into patties, making an indentation in the center of each patty with your thumb (this will help the burger stay flat as it cooks) and flattening the sides of the burgers so that they fit nicely into the air fryer basket.
3. Transfer the burgers to the air fryer basket and air fry for 4 minutes. Flip the burgers over and air fry for another 3 to 4 minutes, until nicely browned and firm to the touch.
4. Serve on soft brioche buns with your choice of topping: lettuce, tomato, red onion, avocado, mayonnaise or mustard

Chapter 5 Vegetarian Mains

Vegetable Burgers

Prep time: 10 minutes / Cook time: 12 minutes
Serves 4

Ingredients :

- 227 g cremini or chestnut mushroomss
- 2 large egg yolks
- ½ medium courgette, trimmed and choppeds
- 60 ml peeled and chopped brown onion
- 1 clove garlic, peeled and finely minceds
- ½ teaspoon salt
- ¼ teaspoon ground black pepper

Preparation Instructions :

1. Place all ingredients into a food processor and pulse twenty times until finely chopped and combined.
2. Separate mixture into four equal sections and press each into a burger shape.
3. Place burgers into ungreased air fryer basket. Adjust the temperature to 192°C and air fry for 12 minutes, turning burgers halfway through cooking. Burgers will be browned and firm when done.
4. Place burgers on a large plate and let cool 5 minutes before serving.

Pesto Vegetable Skewers

Prep time: 30 minutes / Cook time: 8 minutes
Makes 8 skewers

Ingredients :

- 1 medium courgette, trimmed and cut into ½-inch slices
- ½ medium brown onion, peeled and cut into 1-inch squares
- 1 medium red pepper, seeded and cut into 1-inch squares
- 16 whole cremini or chestnut mushroomss
- 80 ml basil pesto
- ½ teaspoon salts
- ¼ teaspoon ground black pepper

Preparation Instructions :

1. Divide courgette slices, onion, and pepper into eight even portions.
2. Place on 6-inch skewers for a total of eight kebabs.
3. Add 2 mushrooms to each skewer and brush kebabs generously with pesto. .Sprinkle each

kebab with salt and black pepper on all sides, then place into ungreased air fryer basket.

4. Adjust the temperature to 192°C and air fry for 8 minutes, turning kebabs halfway through cooking.

5. Vegetables will be browned at the edges and tender-crisp when done. Serve warm.

Potato and Broccoli with Tofu Scramble

Prep time: 15 minutes / Cook time: 30 minutes
Serves 3

Ingredients :

- 600 ml chopped red potato s
- 1 block tofu, chopped finely s
- 1 teaspoon turmeric powder s
- ½ teaspoon garlic powder s
- 1 L broccoli florets

- 2 tablespoons olive oil, divided
- 2 tablespoons tamari
- ½ teaspoon onion powder
- 120 ml chopped onion

Preparation Instructions :

1. Preheat the air fryer to 204°C.
2. Toss together the potatoes and 1 tablespoon of the olive oil.
3. Air fry the potatoes in a baking dish for 15 minutes, shaking once during the cooking time to ensure they fry evenly.
4. Combine the tofu, the remaining 1 tablespoon of the olive oil, turmeric, onion powder, tamari, and garlic powder together, stirring in the onions, followed by the broccoli.
5. Top the potatoes with the tofu mixture and air fry for an additional 15 minutes. Serve warm.

Aubergine and Courgette Bites

Prep time: 30 minutes / Cook time: 30 minutes
Serves 8

Ingredients :

- 2 teaspoons fresh mint leaves, chopped s
- 1½ teaspoons red pepper chilli flakes
- 2 tablespoons melted butters
- 450 g aubergine, peeled and cubed
- 450 g courgette, peeled and cubeds
- 3 tablespoons olive oil

Preparation Instructions :

1. Toss all the above ingredients in a large-sized mixing dish.
2. Roast the aubergine and courgette bites for 30 minutes at 164°C in your air fryer, turning once or twice.

3.Serve with a homemade dipping sauce.

Greek Stuffed Aubergine

Prep time: 15 minutes / Cook time: 20 minutes
Serves 2

Ingredients :

- 1 large aubergines
- 2 tablespoons unsalted butter
- ¼ medium brown onion, diceds
- 60 ml chopped artichoke hearts
- 235 ml fresh spinachs
- 2 tablespoons diced red pepper
- 120 ml crumbled feta

Preparation Instructions :

1.Slice aubergine in half lengthwise and scoop out flesh, leaving enough inside for shell to remain intact.
2.Take aubergine that was scooped out, chop it, and set aside. In a medium skillet over medium heat, add butter and onion. Sauté until onions begin to soften, about 3 to 5 minutes.
3.Add chopped aubergine, artichokes, spinach, and pepper. Continue cooking 5 minutes until peppers soften and spinach wilts.
4.Remove from the heat and gently fold in the feta. Place filling into each aubergine shell and place into the air fryer basket. Adjust the temperature to 160°C and air fry for 20 minutes. Aubergine will be tender when done.
5.Serve warm.

Crispy Cabbage Steaks

Prep time: 5 minutes / Cook time: 10 minutes
Serves 4

Ingredients :

- 1 small head green cabbage, cored and cut into ½-inch-thick slices
- ¼ teaspoon salts
- ¼ teaspoon ground black pepper
- 2 tablespoons olive oils
- 1 clove garlic, peeled and finely minced
- ½ teaspoon dried thymes
- ½ teaspoon dried parsley

Preparation Instructions :

1. Sprinkle each side of cabbage with salt and pepper, then place into ungreased air fryer basket, working in batches if needed.
2. Drizzle each side of cabbage with olive oil, then sprinkle with remaining ingredients on both sides.
3. Adjust the temperature to 176°C and air fry for 10 minutes, turning "steaks" halfway through cooking.
4. Cabbage will be browned at the edges and tender when done.
5. Serve warm.

Cauliflower Rice-Stuffed Peppers

Prep time: 10 minutes / Cook time: 15 minutes
Serves 4

Ingredients :

- 475 ml uncooked cauliflower rices
- 180 ml drained canned petite diced tomatoes
- 2 tablespoons olive oils
- 235 ml shredded Mozzarella cheese
- ¼ teaspoon salts
- ¼ teaspoon ground black pepper
- 4 medium green peppers, tops removed, seeded

Preparation Instructions :

1. In a large bowl, mix all ingredients except peppers. Scoop mixture evenly intopeppers.
2. Place peppers into ungreased air fryer basket. Adjust the temperature to 176°C and air fry for 15 minutes. Peppers will be tender, and cheese will be melted when done.
3. Serve warm.

Roasted Vegetables with Rice

Prep time: 5 minutes / Cook time: 12 minutes
Serves 4

Ingredients :

- 2 teaspoons melted butters
- 235 ml cooked rices
- 1 carrot, choppeds
- 1 garlic clove, minceds
- 2 hard-boiled eggs, grateds
- 235 ml chopped mushrooms
- 235 ml peas
- 1 red onion, chopped
- Salt and black pepper, to taste
- 1 tablespoon soy sauce

Preparation Instructions :

1. Preheat the air fryer to 192°C.

2. Coat a baking dish with melted butter. Stir together the mushrooms, cooked rice, peas, carrot, onion, garlic, salt, and pepper in a large bowl until well mixed.
3. Pour the mixture into the prepared baking dish and transfer to the air fryer basket.
4. Roast in the preheated air fryer for 12 minutes until the vegetables are tender. Divide the mixture among four plates.
5. Serve warm with a sprinkle of grated eggs and a drizzle of soy sauce.

Garlic White Courgette Rolls

Prep time: 20 minutes / Cook time: 20 minutes
Serves 4

Ingredients :

- 2 medium courgettes
- ¼ white onion, peeled and diceds
- 60 ml double creams
- ⅛ teaspoon xanthan gums
- ¼ teaspoon salts
- ¼ teaspoon dried oreganos
- 120 ml sliced baby portobello mushrooms

- 2 tablespoons unsalted butter
- ½ teaspoon finely minced roasted garlic
- 2 tablespoons vegetable broth
- 120 ml full-fat ricotta cheese
- ½ teaspoon garlic powder
- 475 ml spinach, chopped
- 180 ml shredded Mozzarella cheese, divided

Preparation Instructions :

1. Using a mandoline or sharp knife, slice courgette into long strips lengthwise.
2. Place strips between paper towels to absorb moisture. Set aside. In a medium saucepan over medium heat, melt butter.
3. Add onion and sauté until fragrant. Add garlic and sauté 30 seconds. Pour in double cream, broth, and xanthan gum. Turn off heat and whisk mixture until it begins to thicken, about 3 minutes.
4. In a medium bowl, add ricotta, salt, garlic powder, and oregano and mix well.
5. Fold in spinach, mushrooms, and 120 ml Mozzarella. Pour half of the sauce into a round baking pan.
6. To assemble the rolls, place two strips of courgette on a work surface. Spoon 2 tablespoons of ricotta mixture onto the slices and roll up. Place seam side down on top of sauce.
7. Repeat with remaining ingredients. Pour remaining sauce over the rolls and sprinkle with remaining Mozzarella. Cover with foil and place into the air fryer basket. Adjust the temperature to 176°C and bake for 20 minutes.
8. In the last 5 minutes, remove the foil to brown the cheese.
9. Serve immediately.

Cauliflower, Chickpea, and Avocado Mash

Prep time: 10 minutes / Cook time: 25 minutes
Serves 4

Ingredients :

- 1 medium head cauliflower, cut into florets s
- 1 can chickpeas, drained and rinsed
- 1 tablespoon extra-virgin olive oil s
- 2 tablespoons lemon juice
- Salt and ground black pepper, to tastes
- 4 flatbreads, toasted
- 2 ripe avocados, mashed

Preparation Instructions :

Preheat the air fryer to 218°C. In a bowl, mix the chickpeas, cauliflower, lemon juice and olive oil. Sprinkle salt and pepper as desired. Put inside the air fryer basket and air fry for 25 minutes. Spread on top of the flatbread along with the mashed avocado. Sprinkle with more pepper and salt and serve.

Baked Courgette

Prep time: 10 minutes / Cook time: 8 minutes
Serves 4

Ingredients :

- 2 tablespoons salted butters
- 60 ml diced white onion
- ½ teaspoon minced garlics
- 120 ml double cream
- 60 g full fat soft white cheeses
- 235 ml shredded extra mature Cheddar cheese
- 2 medium courgette, spiralized

Preparation Instructions :

1. Preheat the air fryer to 218°C.
2. In a bowl, mix the chickpeas, cauliflower, lemon juice and olive oil.
3. Sprinkle salt and pepper as desired. Put inside the air fryer basket and air fry for 25 minutes.
4. Spread on top of the flatbread along with the mashed avocado.
5. Sprinkle with more pepper and salt and serve.

Rosemary Beetroots with Balsamic Glaze

Prep time: 5 minutes / Cook time: 10 minutes
Serves 2

Ingredients :

Beetroot:
- 2 beetroots, cubeds
- 2 tablespoons olive oil
- 2 sprigs rosemary, choppeds
- Salt and black pepper, to taste

Balsamic Glaze:
- 80 ml balsamic vinegars
- 1 tablespoon honey

Preparation Instructions :

1. Preheat the air fryer to 204°C.
2. Combine the beetroots, olive oil, rosemary, salt, and pepper in a mixing bowl and toss until the beetroots are completely coated.
3. Place the beetroots in the air fryer basket and air fry for 10 minutes until the beetroots are crisp and browned at the edges. Shake the basket halfway through the cooking time.
4. Meanwhile, make the balsamic glaze: Place the balsamic vinegar and honey in a small saucepan and bring to a boil over medium heat. When the sauce starts to boil, reduce the heat to medium-low heat and simmer until the liquid is reduced by half.
5. When ready, remove the beetroots from the basket to a platter. Pour the balsamic glaze over the top and serve immediately.

Broccoli with Garlic Sauce

Prep time: 19 minutes / Cook time: 15 minutes
Serves 4

Ingredients :

- 2 tablespoons olive oil s
- 450 g broccoli florets s
- 2 teaspoons dried rosemary, crushed
- ⅓ teaspoon dried marjoram, crushed
- 80 ml mayonnaise
- Rock salt and freshly ground black pepper, to taste
- Dipping Sauce:
- 3 garlic cloves, minced
- 60 ml sour cream

Preparation Instructions :

1. Lightly grease your broccoli with a thin layer of olive oil. Season with salt and ground black pepper.
2. Arrange the seasoned broccoli in the air fryer basket. Bake at 202°C for 15 minutes, shaking

once or twice.

3. In the meantime, prepare the dipping sauce by mixing all the sauce ingredients.

4. Serve warm broccoli with the dipping sauce and enjoy!

Courgette and Spinach Croquettes

Prep time: 9 minutes / Cook time: 7 minutes
Serves 6

Ingredients :

- 4 eggs, slightly beaten s
- 120 ml goat cheese, crumbled s
- 4 garlic cloves, minceds
- 120 ml Parmesan cheese, grated s
- 450 g courgette, peeled and grateds

- 120 ml almond flour
- 1 teaspoon fine sea salt
- 235 ml baby spinach
- ⅓ teaspoon red pepper flakes
- ⅓ teaspoon dried dill weed

Preparation Instructions :

1. Thoroughly combine all ingredients in a bowl.
2. Now, roll the mixture to form small croquettes. Air fry at 172°C for 7 minutes or until golden.
3. Tate, adjust for seasonings and serve warm.

Baked Turnip and Courgette

Prep time: 5 minutes / Cook time: 15 to 20 minutes
Serves 4

Ingredients :

- 3 turnips, sliceds
- 1 large courgette, sliced
- 1 large red onion, cut into ringss
- 2 cloves garlic, crushed
- 1 tablespoon olive oils
- Salt and black pepper, to taste

Preparation Instructions :

1. Preheat the air fryer to 166°C.
2. Put the turnips, courgette, red onion, and garlic in a baking pan. Drizzle the olive oil over the top and sprinkle with the salt and pepper.
3. Place the baking pan in the preheated air fryer and bake for 15 to 20 minutes, or until the vegetables are tender.
4. Remove from the basket and serve on a plate.

Chapter 6 Vegetables and Sides

Butter and Garlic Fried Cabbage

Prep time: 5 minutes / Cook time: 9 minutes
Serves 2

Ingredients :

- Oil, for spraying
- 2 tablespoons unsalted butter, melted
- ½ teaspoon coarse sea salt
- ½ head cabbage, cut into bite-size pieces
- 1 teaspoon granulated garlic
- ¼ teaspoon freshly ground black pepper

Preparation Instructions :

1. Line the air fryer basket with parchment and spray lightly with oil.
2. In a large bowl, mix together the cabbage, butter, garlic, salt, and black pepper until evenly coated.
3. Transfer the cabbage to the prepared basket and spray lightly with oil.
4. Air fry at 192°C for 5 minutes, toss, and cook for another 3 to 4 minutes, or until lightly crispy.

Brussels Sprouts with Pecans and Gorgonzola

Prep time: 10 minutes / Cook time: 25 minutes
Serves 4

Ingredients :

- 65 g pecans
- 680 g fresh Brussels sprouts, trimmed and quartered
- 2 tablespoons olive oil
- Salt and freshly ground black pepper, to taste
- 30 g crumbled Gorgonzola cheese

Preparation Instructions :

1. Spread the pecans in a single layer of the air fryer and set the heat to 180°C. Air fry for 3 to 5 minutes until the pecans are lightly browned and fragrant. Transfer the pecans to a plate and continue preheating the air fryer, increasing the heat to 200°C.
2. In a large bowl, toss the Brussels sprouts with the olive oil and season with salt and black pepper to taste.
3. Working in batches if necessary, arrange the Brussels sprouts in a single layer in the air fryer basket. Pausing halfway through the baking time to shake the basket, air fry for 20 to 25 minutes until the sprouts are tender and starting to brown on the edges.
4. Transfer the sprouts to a serving bowl and top with the toasted pecans and Gorgonzola. Serve warm or at room temperature.

Gold Artichoke Hearts

Prep time: 15 minutes / Cook time: 8 minutes
Serves 4

Ingredients :

- 12 whole artichoke hearts packed in water, drained
- 60 g plain flour
- 1 egg
- 40 g panko bread crumbs
- 1 teaspoon Italian seasoning
- Cooking oil spray

Preparation Instructions :

1. Squeeze any excess water from the artichoke hearts and place them on paper towels to dry.
2. Place the flour in a small bowl.
3. In another small bowl, beat the egg.
4. In a third small bowl, stir together the panko and Italian seasoning.
5. Dip the artichoke hearts in the flour, in the egg, and into the panko mixture until coated.
6. Insert the crisper plate into the basket and the basket into the unit. Preheat the unit by selecting AIR FRY, setting the temperature to 192°C, and setting the time to 3 minutes. Select START/ STOP to begin.
7. Once the unit is preheated, spray the crisper plate and the basket with cooking oil. Place the breaded artichoke hearts into the basket, stacking them if needed.
8. Select AIR FRY, set the temperature to 192°C, and set the time to 8 minutes. Select START/ STOP to begin.
9. After 4 minutes, use tongs to flip the artichoke hearts. I recommend flipping instead of shaking because the hearts are small, and this will help keep the breading intact. Re-insert the basket to resume cooking. 10. When the cooking is complete, the artichoke hearts should be deep golden brown and crisp. Cool for 5 minutes before serving.

Spicy Roasted Bok Choy

Prep time: 10 minutes / Cook time: 7 to 10 minutes
Serves 4

Ingredients :

- 2 tablespoons olive oil
- 2 teaspoons sesame oil
- 2 cloves garlic, minced
- 2 teaspoons black sesame seeds
- 2 tablespoons reduced-sodium coconut aminos
- 2 teaspoons chili-garlic sauce
- 1 head (about 450 g) bok choy, sliced lengthwise into quarters

Preparation Instructions :

1. Preheat the air fryer to 200°C.
2. In a large bowl, combine the olive oil, coconut aminos, sesame oil, chili-garlic sauce, and garlic. Add the bok choy and toss, massaging the leaves with your hands if necessary, until thoroughly coated.
3. Arrange the bok choy in the basket of the air fryer. Pausing about halfway through the cooking time to shake the basket, air fry for 7 to 10 minutes until the bok choy is tender and the tips of the leaves begin to crisp.
4. Remove from the basket and let cool for a few minutes before coarsely chopping. Serve sprinkled with the sesame seeds.

Roasted Brussels Sprouts with Orange and Garlic

Prep time: 5 minutes / Cook time: 10 minutes
Serves 4

Ingredients :

- 450 g Brussels sprouts, quartered
- 2 garlic cloves, minced
- 2 tablespoons olive oil
- ½ teaspoon salt
- 1 orange, cut into rings

Preparation Instructions :

1. Preheat the air fryer to 180°C.
2. In a large bowl, toss the quartered Brussels sprouts with the garlic, olive oil, and salt until well coated.
3. Pour the Brussels sprouts into the air fryer, lay the orange slices on top of them, and roast for 10 minutes.
4. Remove from the air fryer and set the orange slices aside. Toss the Brussels sprouts before serving.

Simple Cougette Crisps

Prep time: 5 minutes / Cook time: 14 minutes
Serves 4

Ingredients :

- 2 courgette, sliced into ¼- to ½-inch-thick rounds
- ¼ teaspoon garlic granules
- ⅛ teaspoon sea salt
- Freshly ground black pepper, to taste (optional)
- Cooking spray

Preparation Instructions :

1. Preheat the air fryer to 200°C. Spritz the air fryer basket with cooking spray.
2. Put the courgette rounds in the air fryer basket, spreading them out as much as possible. Top with a sprinkle of garlic granules, sea salt, and black pepper (if desired). Spritz the courgette rounds with cooking spray.
3. Roast for 14 minutes, flipping the courgette rounds halfway through, or until the courgette rounds are crisp-tender.
4. Let them rest for 5 minutes and serve.

Garlic-Parmesan Crispy Baby Potatoes

Prep time: 10 minutes / Cook time: 15 minutes
Serves 4

Ingredients :

- Oil, for spraying
- 450 g baby potatoes
- 45 g grated Parmesan cheese, divided
- 3 tablespoons olive oil
- 2 teaspoons garlic powder
- ½ teaspoon onion powder
- ½ teaspoon salt
- ¼ teaspoon freshly ground black pepper
- ¼ teaspoon paprika
- 2 tablespoons chopped fresh parsley, for garnish

Preparation Instructions :

1. Line the air fryer basket with parchment and spray lightly with oil.
2. Rinse the potatoes, pat dry with paper towels, and place in a large bowl.
3. In a small bowl, mix together 45 g of Parmesan cheese, the olive oil, garlic, onion powder, salt, black pepper, and paprika. Pour the mixture over the potatoes and toss to coat.
4. Transfer the potatoes to the prepared basket and spread them out in an even layer, taking care to keep them from touching. You may need to work in batches, depending on the size of your air fryer.
5. Air fry at 200°C for 15 minutes, stirring after 7 to 8 minutes, or until easily pierced with a fork. Continue to cook for another 1 to 2 minutes, if needed.
6. Sprinkle with the parsley and the remaining Parmesan cheese and serve.

Buffalo Cauliflower with Blue Cheese

Prep time: 15 minutes / Cook time: 5 to 7 minutes per batch
Serves 6

Ingredients :

- 1 large head cauliflower, rinsed and separated into small florets
- 1 tablespoon extra-virgin olive oil
- Cooking oil spray
- 190 g nonfat Greek yogurt
- ½ teaspoon hot sauce
- 2 tablespoons crumbled blue cheese
- ½ teaspoon garlic powder
- 80 ml hot wing sauce
- 60 g buttermilk
- 1 celery stalk, chopped

Preparation Instructions :

1. Insert the crisper plate into the basket and the basket into the unit. Preheat the unit by selecting AIR FRY, setting the temperature to192°C, and setting the time to 3 minutes. Select START/STOP to begin.
2. In a large bowl, toss together the cauliflower florets and olive oil. Sprinkle with the garlic powder and toss again to coat.
3. Once the unit is preheated, spray the crisper plate with cooking oil. Put half the cauliflower into the basket.
4. Select AIR FRY, set the temperature to192°C, and set the time to 7 minutes. Select START/ STOP to begin.
5. After 3 minutes, remove the basket and shake the cauliflower. Reinsert the basket to resume cooking. After 2 minutes, check the cauliflower. It is done when it is browned. If not, resume cooking.
6. When the cooking is complete, transfer the cauliflower to a serving bowl and toss with half the hot wing sauce.
7. Repeat steps 4, 5, and 6 with the remaining cauliflower and hot wing sauce.
8. In a small bowl, stir together the yogurt, buttermilk, hot sauce, celery, and blue cheese. Drizzle the sauce over the finished cauliflower and serve.

Garlic Cauliflower with Tahini

Prep time: 10 minutes / Cook time: 20 minutes
Serves 4

Ingredients :

Cauliflower:

- 500 g cauliflower florets (about 1 large head)
- 3 tablespoons vegetable oil
- ½ teaspoon ground coriander
- 6 garlic cloves, smashed and cut into thirds
- ½ teaspoon ground cumin
- ½ teaspoon coarse sea salt

Sauce:

- 2 tablespoons tahini (sesame paste)
- 1 tablespoon fresh lemon juice
- ½ teaspoon coarse sea salt
- 2 tablespoons hot water
- 1 teaspoon minced garlic

Preparation Instructions :

1. For the cauliflower: In a large bowl, combine the cauliflower florets and garlic. Drizzle with the vegetable oil. Sprinkle with the cumin, coriander, and salt. Toss until well coated.
2. Place the cauliflower in the air fryer basket. Set the air fryer to 200ºC for 20 minutes, turning the cauliflower halfway through the cooking time.
3. Meanwhile, for the sauce: In a small bowl, combine the tahini, water, lemon juice, garlic, and salt. (The sauce will appear curdled at first, but keep stirring until you have a thick, creamy, smooth mixture.) 4. Transfer the cauliflower to a large serving bowl. Pour the sauce over and toss gently to coat. Serve immediately.

Green Tomato Salad

Prep time: 10 minutes / Cook time: 8 to 10 minutes
Serves 4

Ingredients :

- 4 green tomatoes
- 1 large egg, lightly beaten
- 1 tablespoon Creole seasoning

Buttermilk Dressing:

- 230 g mayonnaise
- 2 teaspoons fresh lemon juice
- 1 teaspoon dried dill
- ½ teaspoon salt
- ½ teaspoon onion powder

- ½ teaspoon salt
- 50 g peanut flour
- 1 (140 g) bag rocket

- 120 g sour cream
- 2 tablespoons finely chopped fresh parsley
- 1 teaspoon dried chives
- ½ teaspoon garlic powder

Preparation Instructions :

1. Preheat the air fryer to 200ºC.
2. Slice the tomatoes into ½-inch slices and sprinkle with the salt. Let sit for 5 to 10 minutes.
3. Place the egg in a small shallow bowl. In another small shallow bowl, combine the peanut flour and Creole seasoning. Dip each tomato slice into the egg wash, then dip into the peanut flour mixture, turning to coat evenly.
4. Working in batches if necessary, arrange the tomato slices in a single layer in the air fryer basket and spray both sides lightly with olive oil. Air fry until browned and crisp, 8 to 10 minutes.
5. To make the buttermilk dressing: In a small bowl, whisk together the mayonnaise, sour cream, lemon juice, parsley, dill, chives, salt, garlic powder, and onion powder.
6. Serve the tomato slices on top of a bed of the rocket with the dressing on the side.

Lemon-Thyme Asparagus

Prep time: 5 minutes / Cook time: 4 to 8 minutes
Serves 4

Ingredients :

- 450 g asparagus, woody ends trimmed off
- 1 tablespoon avocado oil
- ½ teaspoon dried thyme or ½ tablespoon chopped fresh thyme
- Sea salt and freshly ground black pepper, to taste
- 60 g goat cheese, crumbled
- Zest and juice of 1 lemon
- Flaky sea salt, for serving (optional)

Preparation Instructions :

1. In a medium bowl, toss together the asparagus, avocado oil, and thyme, and season with sea salt and pepper.
2. Place the asparagus in the air fryer basket in a single layer. Set the air fryer to 200°C and air fry for 4 to 8 minutes, to your desired doneness.
3. Transfer to a serving platter. Top with the goat cheese, lemon zest, and lemon juice. If desired, season with a pinch of flaky salt.

Lush Vegetable Salad

Prep time: 15 minutes / Cook time: 10 minutes
Serves 4

Ingredients :

- 6 plum tomatoes, halved
- 4 long red pepper, sliced
- 6 cloves garlic, crushed
- 1 teaspoon paprika
- Salt and ground black pepper, to taste
- 2 large red onions, sliced
- 2 yellow pepper, sliced
- 1 tablespoon extra-virgin olive oil
- ½ lemon, juiced
- 1 tablespoon baby capers

Preparation Instructions :

1. Preheat the air fryer to 220°C.
2. Put the tomatoes, onions, peppers, and garlic in a large bowl and cover with the extra-virgin olive oil, paprika, and lemon juice. Sprinkle with salt and pepper as desired.
3. Line the inside of the air fryer basket with aluminum foil. Put the vegetables inside and air fry for 10 minutes, ensuring the edges turn brown.
4. Serve in a salad bowl with the baby capers.

Rosemary New Potatoes

Prep time: 10 minutes / Cook time: 5 to 6 minutes
Serves 4

Ingredients :

- 3 large red potatoes
- ¼ teaspoon ground rosemary
- ¼ teaspoon ground thyme
- ⅛ teaspoon salt
- ⅛ teaspoon ground black pepper
- 2 teaspoons extra-light olive oil

Preparation Instructions :

1. Preheat the air fryer to 170°C.2. Place potatoes in large bowl and sprinkle with rosemary, thyme, salt, and pepper.
2. Stir with a spoon to distribute seasonings evenly.
3. Add oil to potatoes and stir again to coat well.
4. Air fry at 170°C for 4 minutes. Stir and break apart any that have stuck together.
5. Cook an additional 1 to 2 minutes or until fork-tender.

Zesty Fried Asparagus

Prep time: 3 minutes / Cook time: 10 minutes
Serves 4

Ingredients :

- Oil, for spraying
- 10 to 12 spears asparagus, trimmed
- 2 tablespoons olive oil
- 1 tablespoon garlic powder
- 1 teaspoon chili powder
- ½ teaspoon ground cumin
- ¼ teaspoon salt

Preparation Instructions :

1. Line the air fryer basket with parchment and spray lightly with oil.
2. If the asparagus are too long to fit easily in the air fryer, cut them in half.
3. Place the asparagus, olive oil, garlic, chili powder, cumin, and salt in a zip-top plastic bag, seal, and toss until evenly coated.
4. Place the asparagus in the prepared basket.
5. Roast at 200°C for 5 minutes, flip, and cook for another 5 minutes, or until bright green and

firm but tender.

Mashed Sweet Potato Tots

Prep time: 10 minutes / Cook time: 12 to 13 minutes per batch
Makes 18 to 24 tots

Ingredients :
- 210 g cooked mashed sweet potatoes
- 1 egg white, beaten
- ⅛ teaspoon ground cinnamon
- 1 dash nutmeg
- 2 tablespoons chopped pecans
- 1½ teaspoons honey
- Salt, to taste
- 50 g panko bread crumbs
- Oil for misting or cooking spray

Preparation Instructions :
1. Preheat the air fryer to 200ºC.
2. In a large bowl, mix together the potatoes, egg white, cinnamon, nutmeg, pecans, honey, and salt to taste.
3. Place panko crumbs on a sheet of wax paper.
4. For each tot, use about 2 teaspoons of sweet potato mixture. To shape, drop the measure of potato mixture onto panko crumbs and push crumbs up and around potatoes to coat edges. Then turn tot over to coat other side with crumbs.
5. Mist tots with oil or cooking spray and place in air fryer basket in single layer.
6. Air fry at 200ºC for 12 to 13 minutes, until browned and crispy.
7. Repeat steps 5 and 6 to cook remaining tots.

Beans and Greens Pizza

Prep time: 11 minutes / Cook time: 14 to 19 minutes
Serves 4

Ingredients :

- 180 ml wholemeal pastry flour
- 1 tablespoon olive oil, divided
- 475 ml chopped fresh baby spinach
- 235 ml canned no-added-salt cannellini beans, rinsed and drained
- ½ teaspoon dried thyme
- ½ teaspoon low-salt baking powder
- 235 ml chopped kale
- 1 piece low-salt string cheese, torn into pieces

Preparation Instructions :

1. In a small bowl, mix the pastry flour and baking powder until well combined. Add 60 ml water and 2 teaspoons of olive oil. Mix until a dough forms.
2. On a floured surface, press or roll the dough into a 7-inch round. Set aside while you cook the greens.
3. In a baking pan, mix the kale, spinach, and remaining teaspoon of the olive oil. Air fry at 176°C for 3 to 5 minutes, until the greens are wilted. Drain well.
4. Put the pizza dough into the air fryer basket. Top with the greens, cannellini beans, thyme, and string cheese. Air fry for 11 to 14 minutes, or until the crust is golden brown and the cheese is melted.
5. Cut into quarters to serve.

Avocado and Slaw Tacos

Prep time: 15 minutes / Cook time: 6 minutes
Serves 4

Ingredients :

- 60 ml plain flour
- ¼ teaspoon ground black pepper
- 300 ml panko breadcrumbs
- 2 avocados, peeled and halved, cut into ½-inch-thick slices
- ½ small red cabbage, thinly sliced
- 2 spring onions, thinly sliced
- 60 ml mayonnaise
- 4 corn tortillas, warmed
- Cooking spray
- ¼ teaspoon salt, plus more as needed
- 2 large egg whites
- 2 tablespoons olive oil
- 1 deseeded jalapeño, thinly sliced
- 120 ml coriander leaves
- Juice and zest of 1 lime
- 120 ml sour cream

Preparation Instructions :

1. Preheat the air fryer to 204ºC. Spritz the air fryer basket with cooking spray.
2. Pour the flour in a large bowl and sprinkle with salt and black pepper, then stir to mix well.
3. Whisk the egg whites in a separate bowl. Combine the panko with olive oil on a shallow dish. Dredge the avocado slices in the bowl of flour, then into the egg to coat.
4. Shake the excess off, then roll the slices over the panko.
5. Arrange the avocado slices in a single layer in the basket and spritz the cooking spray. Air fry for 6 minutes or until tender and lightly browned. Flip the slices halfway through with tongs.
6. Combine the cabbage, jalapeño, onions, coriander leaves, mayo, lime juice and zest, and a touch of salt in a separate large bowl. Toss to mix well.
7. Unfold the tortillas on a clean work surface, then spread with cabbage slaw and air fried avocados.
8. Top with sour cream and serve.

Barbecue Pulled Pork Sandwiches

Prep time: 15 minutes / Cook time: 30 minutes
Serves 4

Ingredients :

- 350 ml prepared barbecue sauce
- 2 tablespoons distilled white vinegar
- 2 tablespoons light brown sugar
- 1 tablespoon minced garlic
- 1 teaspoon hot sauce
- 900 g pork shoulder roast
- 1 to 2 tablespoons oil
- 4 sandwich buns

Preparation Instructions :

1. In a medium bowl, stir together the barbecue sauce, vinegar, brown sugar, garlic, and hot sauce.
2. Preheat the air fryer to 182ºC. Line the air fryer basket with parchment paper and spritz it with oil.
3. Place the pork on the parchment and baste it with a thick layer of sauce. Cook for 5 minutes. Flip the pork and baste with sauce.
4. Repeat 3 more times for a total of 20 minutes of cook time, ending with basting.
5. Increase the air fryer temperature to 200ºC. Cook the pork for 5 minutes. Flip and baste. Cook for 5 minutes more. Flip and baste. Let sit for 5 minutes before pulling the pork into 1-inch pieces. Transfer to a bowl and toss the pork with the remaining sauce.
6. Serve on buns.

Mushroom Pitta Pizzas

Prep time: 10 minutes / Cook time: 5 minutes
Serves 4

Ingredients :

- 4 (3-inch) pittas
- 180 ml pizza sauce
- ½ teaspoon dried basil
- 235 ml grated Mozzarella or provolone cheese

- 1 tablespoon olive oil
- 1 (113 g) jar sliced mushrooms, drained
- 2 spring onions, minced
- 235 ml sliced grape tomatoes

Preparation Instructions :

1. Brush each piece of pitta with oil and top with the pizza sauce.
2. Add the mushrooms and sprinkle with basil and spring onions. Top with the grated cheese.
3. Bake at 182ºC for 3 to 6 minutes or until the cheese is melted and starts to brown.
4. Top with the grape tomatoes and serve immediately.

English Muffin Tuna Sandwiches

Prep time: 8 minutes / Cook time: 5 minutes
Serves 4

Ingredients :

- 1 (170 g) can chunk light tuna, drained
- 2 tablespoons mustard
- 2 spring onions, minced
- 3 tablespoons softened butter

- 60 ml mayonnaise
- 1 tablespoon lemon juice
- 3 English muffins, split with a fork
- 6 thin slices provolone or Muenster cheese

Preparation Instructions :

1. In a small bowl, combine the tuna, mayonnaise, mustard, lemon juice, and spring onions.
2. Butter the cut side of the English muffins. Air fry butter-side up in the air fryer at 200ºC for 2 to 4 minutes or until light golden brown.
3. Remove the muffins from the air fryer basket.
4. Top each muffin with one slice of cheese and return to the air fryer. Air fry for 2 to 4 minutes or until the cheese melts and starts to brown.
5. Remove the muffins from the air fryer, top with the tuna mixture, and serve.

Tuna Wraps

Prep time: 10 minutes / Cook time: 4 to 7 minutes
Serves 4

Ingredients :

- 450 g fresh tuna steak, cut into 1-inch cubes
- 2 garlic cloves, minced
- 4 low-salt wholemeal tortillas
- 475 ml shredded romaine lettuce
- 1 tablespoon grated fresh ginger
- ½ teaspoon toasted sesame oil
- 60 ml low-fat mayonnaise
- 1 red pepper, thinly sliced

Preparation Instructions :

1. In a medium bowl, mix the tuna, ginger, garlic, and sesame oil. Let it stand for 10 minutes.
2. Air fry the tuna in the air fryer at 200°C for 4 to 7 minutes, or until done to your liking and lightly browned.
3. Make wraps with the tuna, tortillas, mayonnaise, lettuce, and pepper.
4. Serve immediately.

Korean Flavour Beef and Onion Tacos

Prep time: 1 hour 15 minutes / Cook time: 12 minutes
Serves 6

Ingredients :

- 2 tablespoons gochujang chilli sauce
- 2 tablespoons sesame seeds
- 2 cloves garlic, minced
- 2 teaspoons sugar
- 680 g thinly sliced braising steak
- 6 corn tortillas, warmed
- 120 ml kimchi
- 1 tablespoon soy sauce
- 2 teaspoons minced fresh ginger
- 2 tablespoons toasted sesame oil
- ½ teaspoon rock salt
- 1 medium red onion, sliced
- 60 ml chopped fresh coriander
- 120 ml chopped spring onions

Preparation Instructions :

1. Combine the gochujang, soy sauce, sesame seeds, ginger, garlic, sesame oil, sugar, and salt in a large bowl. Stir to mix well.
2. Dunk the braising steak in the large bowl. Press to submerge, then wrap the bowl in plastic and refrigerate to marinate for at least 1 hour.
3. Preheat the air fryer to 204°C.
4. Remove the braising steak from the marinade and transfer to the preheated air fryer basket.
5. Add the onion and air fry for 12 minutes or until well browned. Shake the basket halfway through.
6. Unfold the tortillas on a clean work surface, then divide the fried beef and onion on the tortillas. Spread the coriander, kimchi, and spring onions on top.
7. Serve immediately.

Cheesy Chicken Sandwich

Prep time: 10 minutes / Cook time: 5 to 7 minutes
Serves 1

Ingredients :

- 80 ml chicken, cooked and shredded
- 1 hamburger bun
- 1 teaspoon mayonnaise
- 1 teaspoon olive oil
- ¼ teaspoon smoked paprika
- ¼ teaspoon garlic powder
- 2 Mozzarella slices
- 60 ml shredded cabbage
- 2 teaspoons butter, melted
- ½ teaspoon balsamic vinegar
- ¼ teaspoon black pepper
- Pinch of salt

Preparation Instructions :

1. Preheat the air fryer to 188ºC.
2. Brush some butter onto the outside of the hamburger bun. In a bowl, coat the chicken with the garlic powder, salt, pepper, and paprika.
3. In a separate bowl, stir together the mayonnaise, olive oil, cabbage, and balsamic vinegar to make coleslaw.
4. Slice the bun in two. Start building the sandwich, starting with the chicken, followed by the Mozzarella, the coleslaw, and finally the top bun. Transfer the sandwich to the air fryer and bake for 5 to 7 minutes.
5. Serve immediately.

Veggie Salsa Wraps

**Prep timeVeggie
Salsa Wraps**

Ingredients :

- 235 ml red onion, sliced
- 1 poblano or Padron pepper, deseeded and finely chopped
- 1 head lettuce
- 227 g Mozzarella cheese
- 1 courgette, chopped
- 120 ml salsa

Preparation Instructions :

1. Preheat the air fryer to 200ºC.
2. Place the red onion, courgette, and pepper in the air fryer basket and air fry for 7 minutes, or until they are tender and fragrant.
3. Divide the veggie mixture among the lettuce leaves and spoon the salsa over the top.
4. Finish off with Mozzarella cheese. Wrap the lettuce leaves around the filling.
5. Serve immediately.

Cheesy Veggie Wraps

**Prep time: 15 minutes / Cook time: 8 to 10 minutes per batch
Serves 4**

Ingredients :

- 227 g green beans
- 1 large red pepper, sliced
- ¼ teaspoon salt
- 3 tablespoons lemon juice
- 4 (6-inch) wholemeal wraps
- 1 lemon, cut into wedges
- 2 portobello mushroom caps, sliced
- 2 tablespoons olive oil, divided
- 1 (425 g) can chickpeas, drained
- ¼ teaspoon ground black pepper
- 110 g fresh herb or garlic goat cheese, crumbled

Preparation Instructions :

1. Preheat the air fryer to 204°C.
2. Add the green beans, mushrooms, red pepper to a large bowl. Drizzle with 1 tablespoon olive oil and season with salt. Toss until well coated.
3. Transfer the vegetable mixture to a baking pan. Air fry in the preheated air fryer in 2 batches, 8 to 10 minutes per batch, stirring constantly during cooking. Meanwhile, mash the chickpeas with lemon juice, pepper and the remaining 1 tablespoon oil until well blended Unfold the wraps on a clean work surface.
4. Spoon the chickpea mash on the wraps and spread all over. Divide the cooked veggies among wraps.
5. Sprinkle 30 g crumbled goat cheese on top of each wrap. Fold to wrap.
6. Squeeze the lemon wedges on top and serve.

Bacon and Pepper Sandwiches

Prep time: 15 minutes / Cook time: 7 minutes
Serves 4

Ingredients :

- 80 ml spicy barbecue sauce
- 8 slices precooked bacon, cut into thirds
- 1 yellow pepper, sliced
- 300 ml torn butterhead lettuce leaves
- 2 tablespoons honey
- 1 red pepper, sliced
- 3 pitta pockets, cut in half
- 2 tomatoes, sliced

Preparation Instructions :

1. In a small bowl, combine the barbecue sauce and the honey.
2. Brush this mixture lightly onto the bacon slices and the red and yellow pepper slices.
3. Put the peppers into the air fryer basket and air fry at 176°C for 4 minutes. Then shake the basket, add the bacon, and air fry for 2 minutes or until the bacon is browned and the peppers are tender.
4. Fill the pitta halves with the bacon, peppers, any remaining barbecue sauce, lettuce, and tomatoes, and serve immediately.

Jerk Chicken Wraps

Prep time: 30 minutes / Cook time: 15 minutes
Serves 4

Ingredients :

- 450 g boneless, skinless chicken tenderloins
- 235 ml jerk marinade
- Olive oil
- 4 large low-carb tortillas
- 235 ml julienned carrots
- 235 ml peeled cucumber ribbons
- 235 ml shredded lettuce
- 235 ml mango or pineapple chunks

Preparation Instructions :

1. In a medium bowl, coat the chicken with the jerk marinade, cover, and refrigerate for 1 hour.
2. Spray the air fryer basket lightly with olive oil. Place the chicken in the air fryer basket in a single layer and spray lightly with olive oil.
3. You may need to cook the chicken in batches. Reserve any leftover marinade.
4. Air fry at 192°C for 8 minutes. Turn the chicken over and brush with some of the remaining marinade. Cook until the chicken reaches an internal temperature of at least 74°C, an additional 5 to 7 minutes.
5. To assemble the wraps, fill each tortilla with 60 ml carrots, 60 ml cucumber, 60 ml lettuce, and 60 ml mango. Place one quarter of the chicken tenderloins on top and roll up the tortilla.
6. These are great served warm or cold.

Shrimp and Grilled Cheese Sandwiches

Prep time: 10 minutes / Cook time: 5 minutes
Serves 4

Ingredients :

- 300 ml shredded Colby, Cheddar, or Havarti cheese
- 1 (170 g) can tiny shrimp, drained
- 3 tablespoons mayonnaise
- 2 tablespoons minced spring onion
- 4 slices wholemeal or wholemeal bread
- 2 tablespoons softened butter

Preparation Instructions :

1. In a medium bowl, combine the cheese, shrimp, mayonnaise, and spring onion, and mix well.

2. Spread this mixture on two of the slices of bread. Top with the other slices of bread to make two sandwiches.
3. Spread the sandwiches lightly with butter.
4. Air fry at 204ºC for 5 to 7 minutes or until the bread is browned and crisp and the cheese is melted.
5. Cut in half and serve warm.

Nugget and Veggie Taco Wraps

Prep time: 5 minutes / Cook time: 15 minutes
Serves 4

Ingredients :

- 1 tablespoon water
- 4 pieces commercial vegan nuggets, chopped
- 1 small brown onion, diced
- 1 small red pepper, chopped
- 2 cobs grilled corn kernels
- 4 large corn tortillas
- Mixed greens, for garnish

Preparation Instructions :

1. Preheat the air fryer to 204ºC.
2. Over a medium heat, sauté the nuggets in the water with the onion, corn kernels and pepper in a skillet, then remove from the heat.
3. Fill the tortillas with the nuggets and vegetables and fold them up.
4. Transfer to the inside of the fryer and air fry for 15 minutes.
5. Once crispy, serve immediately, garnished with the mixed greens.

Mexican Flavour Chicken Burgers

Prep time: 15 minutes / Cook time: 20 minutes
Serves 6 to 8

Ingredients :

- 4 skinless and boneless chicken breasts
- 1 jalapeño pepper
- 1 tablespoon thyme
- 1 tablespoon mustard powder
- 1 egg
- 2 tomatoes, sliced
- 6 to 8 brioche buns, sliced lengthwise
- Cooking spray
- 1 small head of cauliflower, sliced into florets
- 3 tablespoons smoked paprika
- 1 tablespoon oregano
- 1 teaspoon cayenne pepper
- Salt and ground black pepper, to taste
- 2 lettuce leaves, chopped
- 180 ml taco sauce

Preparation Instructions :

1. Preheat the air fryer to 176°C and spritz with cooking spray.
2. In a blender, add the cauliflower florets, jalapeño pepper, paprika, thyme, oregano, mustard powder and cayenne pepper and blend until the mixture has a texture similar to breadcrumbs.
3. Transfer ¾ of the cauliflower mixture to a medium bowl and set aside.
4. Beat the egg in a different bowl and set aside.
5. Add the chicken breasts to the blender with remaining cauliflower mixture. Sprinkle with salt and pepper. Blend until finely chopped and well mixed. Remove the mixture from the blender and form into 6 to 8 patties.
6. One by one, dredge each patty in the reserved cauliflower mixture, then into the egg. Dip them in the cauliflower mixture again for additional coating.
7. Place the coated patties into the air fryer basket and spritz with cooking spray. Air fry for 20 minutes or until golden and crispy. Flip halfway through to ensure even cooking.
8. Transfer the patties to a clean work surface and assemble with the buns, tomato slices, chopped lettuce leaves and taco sauce to make burgers.
9. Serve and enjoy.

Chapter 8 Desserts

Strawberry Pecan Pie

Prep time: 15 minutes / Cook time: 10 minutes
Serves 6

Ingredients :

- 190 g whole shelled pecans
- 240 ml heavy whipping cream
- 2 tablespoons sour cream
- 1 tablespoon unsalted butter, softened
- 12 medium fresh strawberries, hulled

Preparation Instructions :

1. Place pecans and butter into a food processor and pulse ten times until a dough forms. Press dough into the bottom of an ungreased round nonstick baking dish.
2. Place dish into air fryer basket. Adjust the temperature to 160°C and set the timer for 10 minutes. Crust will be firm and golden when done. Let cool 20 minutes.
3. In a large bowl, whisk cream until fluffy and doubled in size, about 2 minutes.
4. In a separate large bowl, mash strawberries until mostly liquid. Fold strawberries and sour cream into whipped cream.
5. Spoon mixture into cooled crust, cover, and place in refrigerator for at least 30 minutes to set. Serve chilled.

Chocolate and Rum Cupcakes

Prep time: 5 minutes / Cook time: 15 minutes
Serves 6

Ingredients :

- 150 g granulated sweetener
- 1 teaspoon unsweetened baking powder
- ½ teaspoon baking soda
- ¼ teaspoon grated nutmeg
- 120 ml milk
- 3 eggs, whisked
- 70 g blueberries
- 140 g almond flour
- 3 teaspoons cocoa powder
- ½ teaspoon ground cinnamon
- ⅛ teaspoon salt
- 110 g butter, at room temperature
- 1 teaspoon pure rum extract
- Cooking spray

Preparation Instructions :

1. Preheat the air fryer to 176°C. Spray a 6-cup muffin tin with cooking spray.
2. In a mixing bowl, combine the sweetener, almond flour, baking powder, cocoa powder, baking soda, cinnamon, nutmeg, and salt and stir until well blended.

3. In another mixing bowl, mix together the milk, butter, egg, and rum extract until thoroughly combined. Slowly and carefully pour this mixture into the bowl of dry mixture. Stir in the blueberries.
4. Spoon the batter into the greased muffin cups, filling each about three-quarters full.
5. Bake for 15 minutes, or until the center is springy and a toothpick inserted in the middle comes out clean.
6. Remove from the basket and place on a wire rack to cool. Serve immediately.

Kentucky Chocolate Nut Pie

Prep time: 20 minutes / Cook time: 25 minutes
Serves 8

Ingredients :

- 2 large eggs, beaten
- 200 g granulated sugar
- 190 g coarsely chopped pecans
- 2 tablespoons bourbon, or peach juice
- 75 g unsalted butter, melted
- 60 g plain flour
- 170 g milk chocolate chips
- 1 (9-inch) unbaked piecrust

Preparation Instructions :

1. In a large bowl, stir together the eggs and melted butter. Add the sugar and flour and stir until combined. Stir in the pecans, chocolate chips, and bourbon until well mixed.
2. Using a fork, prick holes in the bottom and sides of the pie crust. Pour the pie filling into the crust.
3. Preheat the air fryer to 176ºC.
4. Cook for 25 minutes, or until a knife inserted into the middle of the pie comes out clean. Let set for 5 minutes before serving.

Pecan Bars

Prep time: 5 minutes / Cook time: 40 minutes
Serves 12

Ingredients :

- 220 g coconut flour
- 4 tablespoons coconut oil, softened
- 1 egg, beaten
- 5 tablespoons granulated sweetener
- 60 ml heavy cream
- 4 pecans, chopped

Preparation Instructions :

1. Mix coconut flour, sweetener, coconut oil, heavy cream, and egg.
2. Pour the batter in the air fryer basket and flatten well.
3. Top the mixture with pecans and cook the meal at 176ºC for 40 minutes.
4. Cut the cooked meal into the bars.

Peach Fried Pies

Prep time: 15 minutes / Cook time: 20 minutes
Makes 8 pies

Ingredients :

- 420 g can sliced peaches in heavy syrup
- 1 tablespoon cornflour
- Plain flour, for dusting
- 1 teaspoon ground cinnamon
- 1 large egg
- Half a sheet of shortcrust pastry cut into 2

Preparation Instructions :

1. Reserving 2 tablespoons of syrup, drain the peaches well. Chop the peaches into bite-size pieces, transfer to a medium bowl, and stir in the cinnamon.
2. In a small bowl, stir together the reserved peach juice and cornflour until dissolved. Stir this slurry into the peaches.
3. In another small bowl, beat the egg.
4. Dust a cutting board or work surface with flour and spread the piecrusts on the prepared surface. Using a knife, cut each crust into 4 squares (8 squares total).
5. Place 2 tablespoons of peaches onto each dough square. Fold the dough in half and seal the edges. Using a pastry brush, spread the beaten egg on both sides of each hand pie. Using a knife, make 2 thin slits in the top of each pie.
6. Preheat the air fryer to 176°C.
7. Line the air fryer basket with baking paper. Place 4 pies on the baking paper.
8. Cook for 10 minutes. Flip the pies, brush with beaten egg, and cook for 5 minutes more. Repeat with the remaining pies.

Gluten-Free Spice Cookies

Prep time: 10 minutes / Cook time: 12 minutes
Serves 4

Ingredients :

- 4 tablespoons unsalted butter, at room temperature
- 1 large egg
- 240 g almond flour
- 2 teaspoons ground ginger
- ½ teaspoon freshly grated nutmeg
- ¼ teaspoon kosher, or coarse sea salt
- 2 tablespoons agave nectar
- 2 tablespoons water
- 100 g granulated sugar
- 1 teaspoon ground cinnamon
- 1 teaspoon baking soda

Preparation Instructions :

1. Line the bottom of the air fryer basket with baking paper cut to fit.
2. In a large bowl, using a hand mixer, beat together the butter, agave, egg, and water on medium

speed until light and fluffy.

3. Add the almond flour, sugar, ginger, cinnamon, nutmeg, baking soda, and salt. Beat on low speed until well combined.

4. Roll the dough into 2-tablespoon balls and arrange them on the baking paper in the basket. (They don't really spread too much but try to leave a little room between them.) Set the air fryer to 164°C, and cook for 12 minutes, or until the tops of cookies are lightly browned.

5. Transfer to a wire rack and let cool completely. Store in an airtight container for up to a week.

Almond-Roasted Pears

Prep time: 10 minutes / Cook time: 15 to 20 minutes
Serves 4

Ingredients :

Yogurt Topping:
- 140-170 g pot vanilla Greek yogurt
- 2 whole pears
- 1 tablespoon flaked almonds
- ¼ teaspoon almond flavoring
- 4 crushed Biscoff biscuits
- 1 tablespoon unsalted butter

Preparation Instructions :

1. Stir the almond flavoring into yogurt and set aside while preparing pears.
2. Halve each pear and spoon out the core.
3. Place pear halves in air fryer basket, skin side down.
4. Stir together the crushed biscuits and almonds. Place a quarter of this mixture into the hollow of each pear half.
5. Cut butter into 4 pieces and place one piece on top of biscuit mixture in each pear.
6. Roast at 184°C for 15 to 20 minutes, or until pears have cooked through but are still slightly firm.
7. Serve pears warm with a dollop of yogurt topping.

Baked Cheesecake

Prep time: 30 minutes / Cook time: 35 minutes
Serves 6

Ingredients :

- 50 g almond flour
- 2 tablespoons granulated sweetener
- 25 g powdered sweetener
- 1 egg, at room temperature

Topping:
- 355 ml sour cream
- 1 teaspoon vanilla extract
- 1½ tablespoons unsalted butter, melted
- 225 g cream cheese, softened
- ½ teaspoon vanilla paste

- 3 tablespoons powdered sweetener

Preparation Instructions :

1. Thoroughly combine the almond flour, butter, and 2 tablespoons of granulated sweetener in a mixing bowl. Press the mixture into the bottom of lightly greased custard cups.
2. Then, mix the cream cheese, 25 g of powdered sweetener, vanilla, and egg using an electric mixer on low speed. Pour the batter into the pan, covering the crust.
3. Bake in the preheated air fryer at 164°C for 35 minutes until edges are puffed and the surface is firm.
4. Mix the sour cream, 3 tablespoons of powdered sweetener, and vanilla for the topping; spread over the crust and allow it to cool to room temperature.
5. Transfer to your refrigerator for 6 to 8 hours. Serve well chilled.

Glazed Cherry Turnovers

Prep time: 10 minutes / Cook time: 14 minutes per batch
Serves 8

Ingredients :

- 2 sheets frozen puff pastry, thawed
- 2 teaspoons ground cinnamon
- 90 g sliced almonds
- 2 tablespoons milk
- 600 g can premium cherry pie filling
- 1 egg, beaten
- 120 g icing sugar

Preparation Instructions :

1. Roll a sheet of puff pastry out into a square that is approximately 10-inches by 10-inches. Cut this large square into quarters.
2. Mix the cherry pie filling and cinnamon together in a bowl. Spoon ¼ cup of the cherry filling into the center of each puff pastry square. Brush the perimeter of the pastry square with the egg wash. Fold one corner of the puff pastry over the cherry pie filling towards the opposite corner, forming a triangle. Seal the two edges of the pastry together with the tip of a fork, making a design with the tines. Brush the top of the turnovers with the egg wash and sprinkle sliced almonds over each one. Repeat these steps with the second sheet of puff pastry. You should have eight turnovers at the end.
3. Preheat the air fryer to 188°C.
4. Air fry two turnovers at a time for 14 minutes, carefully turning them over halfway through the cooking time.
5. While the turnovers are cooking, make the glaze by whisking the icing sugar and milk together in a small bowl until smooth. Let the glaze sit for a minute so the sugar can absorb the milk. If the consistency is still too thick to drizzle, add a little more milk, a drop at a time, and stir until smooth.
6. Let the cooked cherry turnovers sit for at least 10 minutes. Then drizzle the glaze over each turnover in a zigzag motion. Serve warm or at room temperature.

Peaches and Apple Crumble

Prep time: 10 minutes / Cook time: 10 to 12 minutes
Serves 4

Ingredients :

- 2 peaches, peeled, pitted, and chopped
- 2 tablespoons honey
- 45 g whole-wheat pastry, or plain flour
- 3 tablespoons packed brown sugar
- 1 apple, peeled and chopped
- 45 g quick-cooking oats
- 2 tablespoons unsalted butter, at room temperature
- ½ teaspoon ground cinnamon

Preparation Instructions :

1. Preheat the air fryer to 192°C.
2. Mix together the peaches, apple, and honey in a baking pan until well incorporated.
3. In a bowl, combine the oats, pastry flour, butter, brown sugar, and cinnamon and stir to mix well. Spread this mixture evenly over the fruit.
4. Place the baking pan in the air fryer basket and bake for 10 to 12 minutes, or until the fruit is bubbling around the edges and the topping is golden brown.
5. Remove from the basket and serve warm.

Blueberry Cream Cheese Bread Pudding

Prep time: 15 minutes / Cook time: 1 hour 10 minutes
Serves 6

Ingredients :

- 240 ml single cream
- 65 g granulated sugar, plus 3 tablespoons
- 4 to 5 croissants, cubed
- 110 g cream cheese, cut into small cubes
- 4 large eggs
- 1 teaspoon pure lemon extract
- 150 g blueberries

Preparation Instructions :

1. In a large bowl, combine the cream, eggs, 65 g of sugar, and the extract. Whisk until well combined. Add the cubed croissants, blueberries, and cream cheese. Toss gently until everything is thoroughly combined; set aside.
2. Place a 3-cup Bundt pan (a tube or Angel Food cake pan would work too) in the air fryer basket. Preheat the air fryer to 204°C.
3. Sprinkle the remaining 3 tablespoons sugar in the bottom of the hot pan. Cook for 10 minutes, or until the sugar caramelizes. Tip the pan to spread the caramel evenly across the bottom of the pan.
4. Remove the pan from the air fryer and pour in the bread mixture, distributing it evenly across the pan. Place the pan in the air fryer basket. Set the air fryer to 176°C and bake for 60

minutes, or until the custard is set in the middle. Let stand for 10 minutes before unmolding onto a serving plate.

Cream Cheese Danish

Prep time: 20 minutes / Cook time: 15 minutes
Serves 6

Ingredients :

- 70 g blanched finely ground almond flour
- 140 g full-fat cream cheese, divided
- 75 g powdered sweetener, divided
- 225 g shredded Mozzarella cheese
- 2 large egg yolks
- 2 teaspoons vanilla extract, divided

Preparation Instructions :

1. In a large microwave-safe bowl, add almond flour, Mozzarella, and 30 g cream cheese. Mix and then microwave for 1 minute.
2. Stir and add egg yolks to the bowl. Continue stirring until soft dough forms. Add 50 g sweetener to dough and 1 teaspoon vanilla.
3. Cut a piece of baking paper to fit your air fryer basket. Wet your hands with warm water and press out the dough into a ¼-inch-thick rectangle.
4. In a medium bowl, mix remaining cream cheese, remaining sweetener, and vanilla. Place this cream cheese mixture on the right half of the dough rectangle. Fold over the left side of the dough and press to seal. Place into the air fryer basket.
5. Adjust the temperature to 164°C and bake for 15 minutes.
6. After 7 minutes, flip over the Danish.
7. When done, remove the Danish from baking paper and allow to completely cool before cutting.

Chocolate Soufflés

Prep time: 5 minutes / Cook time: 14 minutes
Serves 2

Ingredients :

- Butter and sugar for greasing the ramekins
- 55 g unsalted butter
- 3 tablespoons granulated sugar
- 2 tablespoons plain flour
- Heavy cream, for serving
- 85 g semi-sweet chocolate, chopped
- 2 eggs, yolks and white separated
- ½ teaspoon pure vanilla extract
- Icing sugar, for dusting the finished soufflés

Preparation Instructions :

1. Butter and sugar two 6-ounce (170 g) ramekins. (Butter the ramekins and then coat the butter with sugar by shaking it around in the ramekin and dumping out any excess.) 2. Melt the

chocolate and butter together, either in the microwave or in a double boiler. In a separate bowl, beat the egg yolks vigorously. Add the sugar and the vanilla extract and beat well again. Drizzle in the chocolate and butter, mixing well. Stir in the flour, combining until there are no lumps.

3. Preheat the air fryer to 164ºC.

4. In a separate bowl, whisk the egg whites to soft peak stage (the point at which the whites can almost stand up on the end of your whisk). Fold the whipped egg whites into the chocolate mixture gently and in stages.

5. Transfer the batter carefully to the buttered ramekins, leaving about ½-inch at the top. (You may have a little extra batter, depending on how airy the batter is, so you might be able to squeeze out a third soufflé if you want to.) Place the ramekins into the air fryer basket and air fry for 14 minutes. The soufflés should have risen nicely and be brown on top. (Don't worry if the top gets a little dark, you'll be covering it with icing sugar in the next step.) 6. Dust with icing sugar and serve immediately with heavy cream to pour over the top at the table.

Shortcut Spiced Apple Butter

Prep time: 5 minutes / Cook time: 1 hour / Makes 1¼ cups

Ingredients :

- Cooking spray
- 130 g packed light brown sugar
- ½ teaspoon kosher, or coarse sea salt
- ⅛ teaspoon ground allspice
- 500 g store-bought unsweetened applesauce
- 3 tablespoons fresh lemon juice
- ¼ teaspoon ground cinnamon

Preparation Instructions :

1. Spray a cake pan with cooking spray. Whisk together all the ingredients in a bowl until smooth, then pour into the greased pan. Set the pan in the air fryer and bake at 172ºC until the apple mixture is caramelized, reduced to a thick purée, and fragrant, about 1 hour.

2. Remove the pan from the air fryer, stir to combine the caramelized bits at the edge with the rest, then let cool completely to thicken. Scrape the apple butter into a jar and store in the refrigerator for up to 2 weeks.

Coconut Macaroons

Prep time: 5 minutes / Cook time: 8 to 10 minutes / Makes 12 macaroons

Ingredients :

- 120 g desiccated, sweetened coconut
- 2 tablespoons sugar
- ½ teaspoon almond extract
- 4½ teaspoons plain flour
- 1 egg white

Preparation Instructions :

1. Preheat the air fryer to 164ºC.

2. In a medium bowl, mix all ingredients together.
3. Shape coconut mixture into 12 balls.
4. Place all 12 macaroons in air fryer basket. They won't expand, so you can place them close together, but they shouldn't touch.
5. Air fry for 8 to 10 minutes, until golden.

Chocolate Chip Cookie Cake

Prep time: 5 minutes / Cook time: 15 minutes
Serves 8

Ingredients :

- 4 tablespoons salted butter, melted
- 1 large egg
- 110 g blanched finely ground almond flour
- 40 g low-carb chocolate chips
- 65 g granular brown sweetener
- ½ teaspoon vanilla extract
- ½ teaspoon baking powder

Preparation Instructions :

1. In a large bowl, whisk together butter, sweetener, egg, and vanilla. Add flour and baking powder and stir until combined.
2. Fold in chocolate chips, then spoon batter into an ungreased round nonstick baking dish.
3. Place dish into air fryer basket. Adjust the temperature to 148°C and set the timer for 15 minutes. When edges are browned, cookie cake will be done.
4. Slice and serve warm.

Pecan Brownies

Prep time: 10 minutes / Cook time: 20 minutes
Serves 6

Ingredients :

- 50 g blanched finely ground almond flour
- 55 g powdered sweetener
- 2 tablespoons unsweetened cocoa powder
- ½ teaspoon baking powder
- 55 g unsalted butter, softened
- 1 large egg
- 35 g chopped pecans
- 40 g low-carb, sugar-free chocolate chips

Preparation Instructions :

1. In a large bowl, mix almond flour, sweetener, cocoa powder, and baking powder. Stir in butter

and egg.

2. Fold in pecans and chocolate chips. Scoop mixture into a round baking pan. Place pan into the air fryer basket.

3. Adjust the temperature to 148°C and bake for 20 minutes.

4. When fully cooked a toothpick inserted in center will come out clean. Allow 20 minutes to fully cool and firm up.

Pumpkin-Spice Bread Pudding

Prep time: 15 minutes / Cook time: 35 minutes
Serves 6

Ingredients :

Bread Pudding:
- 175 ml heavy whipping cream
- 120 g canned pumpkin
- 80 ml whole milk
- 65 g granulated sugar
- 1 large egg plus 1 yolk
- ½ teaspoon pumpkin pie spice
- ⅛ teaspoon kosher, or coarse sea salt
- 1/3 loaf of day-old baguette or crusty country bread, cubed
- 4 tablespoons unsalted butter, melted

Sauce:
- 80 ml pure maple syrup
- 1 tablespoon unsalted butter
- 120 ml heavy whipping cream
- ½ teaspoon pure vanilla extract

Preparation Instructions :

1. For the bread pudding: In a medium bowl, combine the cream, pumpkin, milk, sugar, egg and yolk, pumpkin pie spice, and salt. Whisk until well combined.

2. In a large bowl, toss the bread cubes with the melted butter. Add the pumpkin mixture and gently toss until the ingredients are well combined.

3. Transfer the mixture to a baking pan. Place the pan in the air fryer basket. Set the fryer to 176°C cooking for 35 minutes, or until custard is set in the middle.

4. Meanwhile, for the sauce: In a small saucepan, combine the syrup and butter. Heat over medium heat, stirring, until the butter melts. Stir in the cream and simmer, stirring often, until the sauce has thickened, about 15 minutes. Stir in the vanilla. Remove the pudding from the air fryer.

5. Let the pudding stand for 10 minutes before serving with the warm sauce.

Baked Brazilian Pineapple

Prep time: 10 minutes / Cook time: 10 minutes
Serves 4

Ingredients :

- 95 g brown sugar
- 2 teaspoons ground cinnamon
- 1 small pineapple, peeled, cored, and cut into spears
- 3 tablespoons unsalted butter, melted

Preparation Instructions :

1. In a small bowl, mix the brown sugar and cinnamon until thoroughly combined.
2. Brush the pineapple spears with the melted butter. Sprinkle the cinnamon-sugar over the spears, pressing lightly to ensure it adheres well.
3. Place the spears in the air fryer basket in a single layer. (Depending on the size of your air fryer, you may have to do this in batches.) Set the air fryer to 204°C and cook for 10 minutes for the first batch (6 to 8 minutes for the next batch, as the fryer will be preheated). Halfway through the cooking time, brush the spears with butter.
4. The pineapple spears are done when they are heated through, and the sugar is bubbling. Serve hot.

Grilled Pineapple Dessert

Prep time: 5 minutes / Cook time: 12 minutes
Serves 4

Ingredients :

- Coconut, or avocado oil for misting, or cooking spray
- 4½-inch-thick slices fresh pineapple, core removed
- 1 tablespoon honey
- ¼ teaspoon brandy, or apple juice
- 2 tablespoons slivered almonds, toasted
- Vanilla frozen yogurt, coconut sorbet, or ice cream

Preparation Instructions :

1. Spray both sides of pineapple slices with oil or cooking spray. Place into air fryer basket.
2. Air fry at 200°C for 6 minutes. Turn slices over and cook for an additional 6 minutes.
3. Mix together the honey and brandy.
4. Remove cooked pineapple slices from air fryer, sprinkle with toasted almonds, and drizzle with honey mixture.
5. Serve with a scoop of frozen yogurt or sorbet on the side.

Printed in Great Britain
by Amazon

15851071R10047